GEARS OF GRACE

*There are **Gears of Grace**
that get you to **destiny speed***

LANDEN DORSCH

GEARS OF GRACE
There are Gears of Grace
that get you to destiny speed

Copyright © Landen Dorsch, 2023

Published by Landen Dorsch, Edmonton, Canada

ISBN:
    Paperback   978-1-77354-508-0
       ebook   978-1-77354-509-7

Publication assistance by

PAGEMASTER
PUBLISHING
PageMaster.ca

DEDICATION

Freddie, I love you and miss you so much.
Enjoy Heaven before mom gets there and makes
you renovate.

Acknowledgments

I am so thankful for the many people who have been so gracious to me over the years as I have grown in ministry. This book took longer to write than initially desired as portions needed to be lived out, and so many of you extended grace to me as I learned (and continue to learn) my way through the Gears of Grace. I'm forever grateful for the many relationships that have shaped my life and helped ground me in my journey. I want to thank all those who participated in the endorsements and Paul Fraser for your friendship and for writing the Foreword.

To my staff, thank you for your unwavering commitment to our vision and journey; I love you. Josh and Amy, we have trekked together for many years, and you have been the most incredible partners in ministry and have celebrated every milestone. I can't imagine life and ministry without you. Love you.

I also want to thank my family for their grace and support throughout our ministry adventure. Alyssa and Brody, Tyler and Robin, Amy-Lynn and Jenna, you are my pride and joy; Dad loves you so much. Callum and Silas, Pappy loves you, and to our new little one coming, Pappy can't wait to meet you! My wife Cathy, you are the truest love of my life, my best friend, and the safest place in the world. Elwin and Gloria, this has been a season of new chapters; thank you for loving me as a son.

This acknowledgment is particularly painful as before the publication of Gears of Grace, on Christmas Eve, 2022, my dad, Fred, passed away. He was more than a dad; he was my friend, confidant, cheerleader, and safe harbor. His absence leaves such a large hole in our hearts. And we miss him. My mom, Diana, has been unwavering in her love, support, and encouragement to me and our whole family in how a true disciple of Jesus mourns loss and courageously faces the future. Mom, you inspire us daily to be more like Jesus; I love you so very much.

Genevieve, thank you for your hard work editing and for giving such profound insight, advice, and encouragement. Thank you Dale and the Pagemaster team for your hard work getting Gears of Grace to print. Thank you also to those who shared their stories of shifting gears with all of us.

To my Gateway Family, thank you so much; I love being your Pastor.

And, of course, Jesus, without whom none of this happens.

FOREWORD

A TRADITION HAS EVOLVED FOR LANDEN, ME, AND OUR FRIEND Jeremy to go backcountry fly fishing in the beautiful foothills of western Alberta in the first week of August. This past trip, we were fishing a large, deep pool on an unnamed river (to which we've all been sworn to secrecy), where all three of us could be fishing without tangling lines. It was a beautiful day for fishing, and we were already several hours into our excursion.

Suddenly, I heard Landen yell, "Fish on!" so I pulled my line out of the water to avoid tangling up with Landen's fish. After about ten minutes of Landen fighting the fish to tire it out, it looked like he was about to land that monster. So I made another cast to get back at fishing. Unexpectedly, twenty feet away, I heard the buzz of Landen's reel spinning as the giant cutthroat trout went on another run, with more of the line streaming toward where I had just cast my pheasant tail nymph. Just then, I felt something on my line. "Fish on!" I yelled, thinking I had a large fish as well. It only took a short moment to discover that we had hooked the same fish.

I'm not sure what the Laws of Fishing are to determine a ruling on whose fish it should be, but I think the "Law of First Hooked" came into play that day. So I let out my line so Landen could reel the fish in and net it. Just as the Mighty Fisherman reached out with his net, the trout he'd worked so hard to land shook the hook out of its mouth and skirted back into the deep water. Landen's bad luck became my opportunity, as my hook was still firmly embedded in the fish's mouth. I quickly reeled in this tired-out trout, scooped it up in my net, declaring what an amazing catch I had just landed, and we all had a huge laugh.

I wish I could say that was the only line I have ever taken from my friend Landen, but as a fellow pastor and communicator, I have been stealing his lines for years. His way of taking deep theological truths and making them profoundly understandable is often too good for me to leave out of my sermons. As you read this book, I know you will also take some of his lines. (I just hope you do a better job of referencing him than I have done!)

Twenty years of friendship provide the privilege to walk through the many stages of life together and allow for front-row seats to each other's lives. When you journey through life with someone, you can see if they practice what they preach. I've had many opportunities to see into Landen's life. From watching our kids grow up and get married, doing ministry events together, persevering through tough times, and celebrating the good seasons. I have keenly observed and thoughtfully reflected on this, and he certainly does practice what he preaches. Maybe it's consistency that I've learned the most from him. His big love for his God, his family, his friends, and the Church have not changed -he has stayed the course through thick and thin. My wife and I now sit in the third row at the Church he leads, and we proudly watch as he continues to live courageously and consistently in the call God has given him.

In Gears of Grace, Landen's second book, I find myself positioned as a student taking a self-directed course. I'm highlighting lines for my future sermons, reflecting on new perspectives shared, wrestling with the questions at the end of each chapter, and digging into what he describes in the book as the "Speed of Destiny ."

This idea of the Speed of Destiny and shifting the right gears to get there has me hungry to implement what he's teaching. Landen writes with both strong Biblical structure and clear instruction. He makes the Speed of Destiny seem reachable when so many may perceive it as unattainable. I mean, to fully live in God's greatest purposes can seem impossible at times, right!? But Landen, led by the Spirit, walks us beautifully through the Gears of Grace, helping us to see how God is at work. With each chapter, he guides the reader towards engaging each gear on the way to reaching God's Speed of Destiny for each of us.

As I said before, I have adventured with my friend for many years. I have watched him live out this book. Flipping through its pages, I can see how this book has mirrored much of Landen's life and ministry journey. He's not writing about a theoretical pilgrimage, but rather, one of lived experience firmly supported by Biblical foundation. I have had the privilege of seeing Landen go at the Speed of Destiny. To me, this book is another example of what that looks like for him.

If you are ready for a challenge and change, this book is right for you. Where others may be apprehensive about speaking to certain erroneous thinking in the Church at large, Landen -with his gentle, uncritical teaching pattern --speaks clearly and prophetically to the errors of some of our theology and tradition around grace and purpose. As I've read this book, shifting through the gears of grace, I have had to readjust some thinking in my life. I hope you will read it with expectancy, ready to receive what the Spirit is saying throughout the pages of this book.

Proverbs 2:1-5 (NIV)

"My son, if you accept my words and store up my commands within you, turning your ear to wisdom and applying your heart to understanding-indeed, if you call out for insight and cry aloud for understanding, and if you look for it as for silver and search for it

as hidden treasure, then you will understand the fear
of the Lord and find the knowledge of God."

Philippians 4:8 (NIV)
"Finally, brothers and sisters, whatever is true,
whatever is noble, whatever is right, whatever is pure,
whatever is lovely, whatever is admirable-if anything
is excellent or praiseworthy-think about such things.
Whatever you have learned or received or heard from
me or seen in me-put it into practice. And the God of
peace will be with you."

As you make your way through this book, I pray that you don't just read the words on the pages but also listen for the Spirit leading about your own Speed of Destiny. Gears of Grace is not a book to be finished quickly. Instead, read intentionally and thoughtfully to see how God will speak to you line by line. So, do yourself a favour and don't rush through the timely work my friend has written so beautifully. I know you will be blessed.

Paul Fraser
National Church Multiplication Co-ordinator
for Pentecostal Assemblies of Canada (PAOC)

CONTENTS

INTRODUCTION

2 Corinthians 3:18 (ESV)[1]

*And we all, with unveiled face, beholding the glory of the Lord, are **being transformed** into the same image **from one degree of glory to another.** For this comes from the Lord, who is the Spirit.*

WELCOME TO THE JOURNEY OF THE DISCIPLE. BECAUSE THAT'S what discipleship is: a journey. We journey in our growth until we are called home. But, even then, I believe we will continue to discover and be awestruck as our Heavenly Father reveals the unending glory of His nature to us for all of eternity.

However, determining where we are in our journey can be challenging. We tend to measure our maturity against the perceived maturity of our surrounding brothers and sisters. This sometimes leads to a competitive, insecure, religious environment robbing us of peace, joy, and family.

The purpose of this book is to give readers a sense of where they are in their journey by the revelation, or, Gear of Grace, they are living in, allowing them to consciously pursue their maturation process in the Lord.

We will delve into this in greater detail throughout this book, but in the same way a vehicle's potential for speed is limited by the gear it is in, a Christ follower's potential for mission, purpose, and destiny is limited by their revelation of grace. And like the tension felt in a vehicle at the end of a gear's capacity, when we don't "shift gears" in our understanding of grace, we too live feeling like we are continually bumping up against a glass ceiling. This process leaves us frustrated and unfulfilled. We are aware there is more of God's purposes and anointing available to us but are unable to take hold of it.

By way of a short example, the first Gear of Grace is God's delight to extend mercy. However, this wonderful gift of God allows for sin to remain tolerated in the life of a disciple, limiting their capacity for destiny and purpose to the glass ceiling of sin's authority in their lives. Submission to the lordship of Jesus acts like a clutch, where we choose to "submit to God, resist the Devil and he will flee" (James 4:7), allowing us to "shift" into the next revelation of Grace, managing liberty.

Understanding the Gear of Grace we're in at any particular time, and what's causing the tension of bumping up against the glass ceiling, and the "clutch" that will move us into the next gear, will open entirely new partnerships with God as we mature in Christ.

Ephesians 4:13-15
Until we all attain to the unity of the faith and of the knowledge of the Son of God, to mature manhood, to the measure of the stature of the fullness of Christ, so that we may no longer be children, tossed to and fro by the waves and carried about by every wind of doctrine, by human cunning, by craftiness in deceitful schemes. Rather, speaking the truth in love, we are to grow up in every way into him who is the head, into Christ.

CHAPTER 1

COMPREHENDING GRACE

GRACE. IT'S AN UNFATHOMABLE SUBJECT. ANYONE WHO teaches that they completely understand the nature of God's grace is being untruthful, or in the words of Wesley in *The Princess Bride*, is "trying to sell you something." When Paul wrote to the Ephesians, he specified what the capacity of Grace is.

> *Ephesians 2:6-9*
> *And [God] raised us up with Him and seated us with Him in the heavenly places in Christ Jesus, so that in the coming ages **He might show the immeasurable riches of His Grace in kindness toward us in Christ Jesus. For by grace, you have been saved through faith.** And this is not your own doing; it is the gift of God, not a result of works, so that no one may boast.*

Grace is immeasurable. It will be something we marvel at for the rest of eternity. It is a component of the infinite nature of our Heavenly Father and, therefore, cannot be fully understood, only accepted. And frankly, it leaves us dumbfounded.

SPIRITUAL NEAR SIGHTEDNESS

Our modern Christianity has a dysfunction, resulting in what I would call "Spiritual Near Sightedness." It is a habit of trying to look at God with our natural nearsighted eyes, forgetting that He is infinite. This results in unbelief.

> *Mark 9:22-24*
>
> *"And it has often cast him into fire and into water, to destroy him. But if you can do anything, have compassion on us and help us." And Jesus said to him, "'If you can'! All things are possible for one who believes." Immediately the father of the child cried out and said, "I believe; help my unbelief!"*

How many times has this been the cry of your heart?

"I believe; help my unbelief!"

I'm so thankful for the transparency of the father of this boy. For so many of us, our belief is corrupted by our unbelief because we haven't accepted what we can't understand.

God is infinite.

I can't comprehend the word *infinite*. It means limitless or endless, and impossible to measure or calculate. For example, today's billionaires, even though they possess outrageous wealth, can still exhaust it. And while it would take some imagination, I can see myself being able to drain a billionaire's bank account given the opportunity. Yet with the infinite, there is no possibility of exhausting the resource.

Like outer space, the thought of something being infinite confuses our finite minds. It can't be understood; it can only be accepted.

In the same way, God, who is infinite in love and resource, can't be understood, just simply accepted.

Faith, at its core, is the acceptance of the infiniteness of God. Faith acts as a lens, helping us to see His infinite nature by correcting our nearsightedness. Unbelief views God through unreliable eyes.

Unbelief views God through unreliable eyes.

We must view the attributes of God through faith, which is the lens for His infiniteness. This means the fullness of His nature can't be wholly understood, only accepted by faith. And our response in faith allows our access to the immeasurable.

This incredible grace woven in the personality of our God, who is love, leaves me breathless. I don't deserve His favour; I can't earn it, yet through Jesus I can revel in it, and I'm astounded that it's been given to me. This grace gives me access to the fullness of an immeasurable King.

However, as in all things of God's Kingdom, our capacity to reap the benefits of any Kingdom principle is directly proportional to our revelation of the King regarding that principle. Revelation isn't knowledge alone. Yes, the Holy Spirit awakens us to a fresh understanding of a subject through revelation, but faith activates the benefits of that revelation. Revelation isn't just acquired knowledge; it's applied knowledge through faith.

LOST AND HIDING

For example, years back, I ran a summer camp which was situated in the wilderness and one of my daughters wandered off into the woods and we couldn't find her. After a frantic search of the grounds, I took an ATV and searched for her, calling out her name over and over. I began to despair, wondering if my little girl would be lost in the over seven hundred acres of wilderness.

I drove the ATV back to the main lodge, and to my relief, saw her walking hand in hand with a staffer who'd found her. After wrapping her up in my arms and giving her a big hug and kiss, I asked her if she had heard me calling her name over and over. She looked at me with her big beautiful eyes and said, "I heard you calling daddy, but I thought you were angry and I was afraid so I hid." Her words hit me like a ton of bricks, and I had a revelation of God's love for me in that moment.

"I'm not angry, don't hide."

I've learned to apply that revelation of God's heart for me when I've fallen into the temptation of sin. It's not something I do by feeling, but by faith in His goodness.

LIFE IS A HIGHWAY

Tom Cochrane wrote a song by this name years back. Great tune. I would like to use a highway as a metaphor for the will of God.

Your Father's greatest desire for you is to have an intimate relationship with Him. Everything is born out of that relationship. We often think of the destiny of God as being a destination. However, our destiny is to have an intimate life journey with Jesus. All other pit stops along the highway are opportunities to bring His Kingdom to those places. Jesus didn't die on the Cross just to give us assignments—He died to establish a relationship.

Pursuing God's will as if it were a destination allows us to pick and choose where we will be "Kingdom-like." People "living in" the will of God actively "live out" His Kingdom ways everywhere they go. In other words, they're living an intimate journey with Jesus everywhere.

Matthew 6:9-10

Pray then like this: "Our Father in heaven, hallowed be your name. Your Kingdom come, your will be done, on earth as it is in heaven."

Much has been written/spoken on recently regarding this portion of the Lord's Prayer. The will of God is supposed to look like heaven has come to earth. When Jesus sent his disciples out to heal, He told them to tell those healed that the Kingdom had come near to them. This is His will for you to bring heaven to where you live, where you go, where you work, and who you love.

This is our assignment. It is a lifestyle, not a role.

Matthew 13:33

*He told them another parable. "The **Kingdom of heaven is like leaven** that a woman took and hid in three measures of flour, till it was all leavened."*

Jesus said the Kingdom of Heaven, like leaven, has the properties to affect and transform every aspect of our lives. In many parables, Jesus revealed how the Kingdom of heaven should manifest in our daily lives.

Yes, we have callings and roles in the Kingdom; however, this thinking has relegated ministry to ministers only. As a result, the equippers of Ephesians 4 do the work of the ministry rather than equipping the saints for it.

Ephesians 4:11-12

*And he gave [equippers], the apostles, the prophets, the evangelists, the shepherds and teachers, **to equip the saints for the work of ministry,** for building up the body of Christ.*

The Speed of Destiny

On a highway, you're supposed to travel at highway speed. So, I'd like to introduce the phrase "destiny speed" into our conversation as we journey through the Gears of Grace.

You can't reach highway speed in first gear when driving. Like I said earlier, your access to the benefits of any Kingdom principle depends on your revelation of the King over that principle. Or, for our conversation, the Gear of Grace you are using. Therefore, you can't go at "destiny speed" in the first gear of revelation of the principles of grace.

Your revelation and response to the grace of God will determine your speed on this intimate journey with Jesus.

Counterfeits and Gladiators

Two separate encounters with God birthed this book.

The first encounter was in prayer as I mulled over thoughts with The Lord. I was working on some remarks regarding the counterfeits of the enemy. You see, Satan cannot create. He only perverts. Counterfeits look the same as the original item, masquerading as having the same value as that item. My friends Ken and Jeanne Harrington often speak on counterfeits by saying that no one counterfeits a three-dollar bill because they don't exist. The enemy looks at different aspects of the Kingdom and counterfeits them to confuse the believer so that the believer misrepresents the Kingdom to the world. The Lord was showing me other principles that the enemy had counterfeited to bring confusion to the world regarding God's nature. Things like religion as a counterfeit of holiness. Another was happiness as a counterfeit of joy. Then He talked of tolerance being a counterfeit of grace.

Romans 6:1-2

*What shall we say, then? Are we to **continue in sin***
***that grace may abound? By no means!** How can we*
who died to sin still live in it?

There is a difference between being enabled and being empowered. Tolerance operates from enablement. Enablement permits you to remain in your bondage; empowerment equips you to overcome it.

The world has its view of tolerance, which I will not go on to explain. However, many in the body of Christ understand God's grace as His tolerance, which I must explain. Grace is not an expression of God's tolerance. Grace is the love motivation behind God's redemption. His holiness forbids the tolerance of sin. Redeeming us through the sacrifice of Jesus has satisfied His holiness. We don't mistake grace for mercy. Mercy is not getting what you do deserve, grace is getting what you don't deserve. Grace restores us to return to the point where we lost our way and allows us to build again with the wisdom gained as a result of our mistakes. We are empowered to move forward from our last place of God's favour to follow Him to the next one. Fully forgiven, fully restored and completely secure as children in His family.

WHO AM I?

In 1960, PD Eastman published a children's book called "Are You My Mother?" In it, a little chick hatches while its mother is away, and knowing that he isn't supposed to be alone, the little chick declares he will find his mother and searches for her. After searching amongst some other animals, and them saying they are not his mother, he then asks a car, a boat, and a plane, who, of course, have no answer. Finally, he ends up in a backhoe and asks if it is his mother; it shudders to life with a "snort." The little chick declares, "You're not my mother. You're a snort." Trapped in the "snort's" shovel, he cries, "I want my mother!" as the shovel lifts the chick to his nest and drops him in. Then his mother arrives, and he says, "I know who YOU are. You are a bird, and you are my mother."

Like the little chick, humanity knows deep down that we are made in the image of something. But because of sin, we become estranged from our Father. Many will go from sin to sin, from lie to lie, asking if we are made in that image, searching for our true identity. God's grace shown to us through the Cross, like the "snort", lifts us to our seats in heavenly places, where we can see our Father and say, "I know who YOU are." Grace lets us see that we look just like our Father.

Tolerance enables you to accept your bondage as your identity. Grace empowers you to accept your identity in Christ: a child of God.

The second motivation behind writing this came from a recent dream.

I was in a mansion with many rooms. An angel was leading me through some hallways. The first room I came into was a large open-air room. It was ancient and had sand on the floor. It was sunlit and appeared like an ancient Roman *ludus*, or gladiators training facility. Those in the room were dressed either in old robes, like those worn in that day, or in Roman armour. There was fellowship in the room but also a palpable sense of tension. People were eating together, but they were arguing with one another. Those in armour looked like they were practicing for battle but were using real swords. In their practice, they were nicking each other with their swords, and many were bleeding. None of the injuries looked severe, but they were hurting one another. I found this strange. Also, I noticed they were drinking out of old wine-skins.

The angel led me to another door, which led to a long, green hallway. As I walked down the hallway, I could hear singing. I opened the door at the end of the hallway and entered another large room with a big window; the walls were painted a pleasant green and instead of sand, the floor was carpeted. A smaller group of about fifty people were there, sitting in chairs, and three people were leading worship with guitars. The atmosphere of this room was far more pleasant than the other room. The worship came to a close, and one of the leaders looked at me and said, "Brother, what has God said to you?" I asked for a moment to think and went into a side room with the angel. As I prayed, I heard the Spirit of the Lord say, "You just left the room of restitution and came into the room of family."

Then I awoke.

While I am sure there is more to this dream, the initial broad-stroke revelations that came to me revolved around the two vastly different rooms of restitution and family.

The tension was palpable in the room of restitution filled with gladiators. Gladiators don't fight for a cause like soldiers. They fight each other for entertainment; not for their own entertainment, but for the entertainment of Caesar.

One definition for restitution is the return of something to its original state. The gladiators, drinking from the old wine-skin of religion, fought amongst themselves, arguing and nicking each other with their swords. Far too often, well-meaning believers live using their "swords" to injure one another as they religiously try to return to our original sinless state. As if arguing and infighting could ever bring us into the righteous condition necessary to have a relationship with God.

The second, more pleasant room of family was filled first with worship, love, connection, and then with revelation. It was a room filled with grace.

"Brother, what has God said to you?"

The urgent desire to know what God is saying to us for joint discovery and deeper relationship with Him, is the healthy way for us as a family to engage heaven.

This is important because God did not redeem us for the sake of us entertaining Him. In fact, in that old room of restitution, I believe the enemy, like a Caesar, sits watching us wound one another, thoroughly entertained, as our vain attempts at self-righteousness fall short, and the mission of heaven remains unmet.

God doesn't want to engage us this way; He wants us to be family.

Romans 8:15-17a

For you did not receive the spirit of slavery to fall back into fear, but you have received the Spirit of adoption as sons, by whom we cry, "Abba! Father!" The Spirit himself bears witness with our spirit that we are children of God, and if children, then heirs— heirs of God and fellow heirs with Christ.

Paul purposefully used the image of adoption, writing to the Romans, as it revealed the desire of God's heart to bring us into family. Therefore, possessing clarity on God's desire for family is vital for us to completely experience His grace.

Grace and the Covenant

John 3:16-18

For God so loved the world, that he gave his only Son, that whoever believes in him should not perish but have eternal life. For God did not send his Son into the world to condemn the world, but in order that the world might be saved through him. Whoever

*believes in him is not condemned, but whoever does
not believe is condemned already because he has not
believed in the name of the only Son of God.*

The centrality of the Cross for humanity is paramount. It's the sealing agent that forever represents God's covenant offered to the human race. The entire history and future of humanity's condition rests on the Cross. The first and most powerful message of the grace of God is found in the proclamation of this great news to fallen man: "You have been redeemed! Come and get it!" Whether one chooses redemption or not is left to the exercising of each individual's free will.

> *The centrality of the
> Cross for humanity
> is paramount.
> It's the sealing
> agent that forever
> represents God's
> covenant offered to
> the human race.*

One may ask how a loving God can let people go to hell? My response is, why would any sane person refuse their redemption and *choose* hell?

Deuteronomy 30:19
*I call heaven and earth to witness against you today
that I have set before you life and death, blessing
and curse. Therefore, choose life that you and your
offspring may live.*

THE COVENANT: THE CROSS

Colossians 1:19-20
*For in him all the fullness of God was pleased to
dwell, and through him to reconcile to himself all*

*things, whether on earth or in heaven, **making peace***
by the blood of his Cross.

The reason that I want to spend time first to explore the covenant of the Cross is that our entire revelation of grace depends upon our revelation of the covenant of the Cross. Our lives will always reflect the extent of our revelation because you can only live in the measure you understand. Our life messages reflect what's revealed to us. That is why it is necessary to continue to pursue and grow in all aspects of our faith. We never just arrive; we continue to grow with this never-ending God.

There is a blind spot in the charismatic expression of the body of Christ. It is where we swing to extremes in engaging revelation. I can look back to seasons where faith teaching became the "now" word for the body, and we would swing out to the inevitable excesses that would result. Then declaration became the new word, and again, we would swing out to the excesses. Then to prosperity, then to deliverance, and so on and so on. None of the previously mentioned revelations are bad by any means. They are important and meant to propel the church into new realms of authority, power, grace, and intimacy. But because of swinging out to the excesses of revelations, we end up facing the inevitable dysfunctions from those excesses. As a result, the revelation is either neutered or abandoned in an effort to return to what would seem acceptable.

In our present day, there has been a fresh release of revelation about grace. However, unfortunate excesses have resulted because of the blind spot to swing to extremes. This robs the body of the beauty of holiness because of the permissive tone of tolerance taken by exercising our "freedom in Christ." And so, in response to the excesses of the holiness movement, which led to legalism, we have this swing to excesses in grace, leading to permissiveness.

So, like a swing moving from one apex to the next, our misuse of revelation makes us determined to come into what we would call a "balanced" expression. But we have come down to the lowest point between the two.

Generally, at the bottom of the swing pattern, we are left in a powerless expression between two extremes.

GRACE AND THE SPIRIT OF RELIGION

Here is the point. There are ditches on either side of the road. So, in one ditch, we have religious holiness, which is a massive misrepresentation of true holiness, trapping people under a religious yoke of heaviness, where the level of their performance determines the level of their acceptance by God. However, in the other ditch, we have permissive grace. This is another massive misrepresentation of God's grace, where people are confused about acceptable or unacceptable behaviours. The results are either people performing to be accepted or demanding the acceptance of sinful behaviour.

Both are wrong, and both are religious. At its root, religion requires performance for acceptance. And it is found lurking in the weeds in both ditches.

JESUS: THE RADICAL CENTRIST

Joshua 5:13-15
*When Joshua was by Jericho, he lifted up his eyes and looked, and behold, **a man was standing before him with his drawn sword in his hand**. And Joshua went to him and said to him, "Are you for us, or for our adversaries?" And he said, "No, but I am the commander of the army of the Lord. Now I have come." And Joshua fell on his face to the earth and worshiped and said to him, "What does my lord*

say to his servant?" And the commander of the Lord's
army said to Joshua, "Take off your sandals from your
feet, for the place where you are standing is holy."
And Joshua did so.

Scholars agree that Joshua was having an encounter with Jesus. The fact that the Man didn't prohibit Joshua from worshiping Him points to Him being more than an angel.

This scripture points to the agenda of Jesus, which is the agenda of His Father.

John 5:19

So Jesus said to them, "Truly, truly, I say to you, the
Son can do nothing of his own accord, but only what
he sees the Father doing. For whatever the Father
does, the Son does likewise."

The danger of the blindspots from swinging to extremes is we want to have Jesus join our doctrinal stance and declare others wrong. Regardless of the goodness of the revelation, Jesus will always remain a radical centrist. He can be at the extreme expression of any revelation and isn't defined by it. Because of His submission to His Father, He is not at risk of excesses resulting from its extreme expression.

That radical way of living is meant to be our lifestyle as well.

Joshua asked, "Are you for us or our enemies?" The man's response is impressive; "No, but as commander of the army of the Lord, I have come."

Jesus, are you for us or our enemies? Neither I am for God.
Are you for the right or the left? Neither I am for God.
Are you conservative or liberal? Neither I am for God.
Are you a capitalist or socialist? Neither I am for God.

Our mistake is that we think Jesus can be pigeonholed into an ideology when, in fact, He is prepared to express the love of God in whatever fashion necessary to advance the agenda of His Father. Read through the life of Jesus in the Gospels and see how Jesus couldn't be labelled by any one ideology. He would embrace whatever ideology promoted the agenda of His Father at any time. He held obedience in higher esteem than any party platform.

Instead of a swing, we should think of revelation as a kite. Kites are made to fly, but they fly because they catch the wind. However, without being anchored, the kite may catch the wind but will not be sustained by the wind and eventually fall to the ground. So too, revelation is meant to catch the power of the wind of the Holy Spirit, allowing us to fly at great altitudes and express fresh anointings. However, to live out this revelation for its full potential, it MUST be anchored to the Cross, the covenant of God, for mankind.

This is why we must understand and live in the wonder of this gospel covenant. The potency of the touch of God on our lives depends on it. The greater the length of the string, the higher the kite can fly. The greater the breadth of our revelation of the Cross, the greater the access to the power released through revelation.

One of the most influential books on the covenant of the gospel for me has been Malcolm Smith's book, *The Power of the Blood Covenant*. I would like to briefly examine three examples from his book to help us get a more excellent glimpse of the nature of the covenant of the Cross.

The definition of covenant within the biblical context is crucial for us to understand the fullness of our relationship with God. It is insufficient to view the concept of biblical covenant through the modern lens of a contract. This is what is normal to a Western mindset and so the word covenant is perceived simply as an agreement between two parties in the exchange of goods or services. This kind of understanding drastically reduces the power of the covenant. It is much more than a contract.

Smith defines covenant as "A binding, unbreakable obligation between two parties, based on unconditional love, sealed by love and sacred oath, that creates a relationship in which each party is bound by specific undertakings on each other's behalf. Furthermore, the parties to the covenant place themselves under the penalty of divine retribution should they later attempt to avoid those undertakings. It is a relationship that can be broken only by death."[3]

A beautiful definition, but quite a mouthful. In preparing to speak on this subject, I prayed into this definition and reduced it to a more memorable statement.

A covenant is an unbreakable promise because of unconditional love.

Smith uses examples to help us understand the nature of a covenant found in the Old Testament, one in the life of Abram and two in the life of David.

THE KEEPER OF THE COVENANT

First, Smith helps us understand how a covenant is made. To understand how covenant is made, we first must understand who the keeper of the covenant is.

In Genesis 15, God is making a covenant with Abram about his offspring.

> *Genesis 15:5*
>
> *And he brought him outside and said, "**Look toward heaven, and number the stars, if you are able to number them**." Then he said to him, "**So shall your offspring be**."*

So, God tells Abram to get animals to perform a covenant between them. The custom of the day was to cut the animals in two and separate the halves and walk through them, symbolizing walking through death for the sake of the promise they were making.

Abram waits for God to show up to participate in the covenant together, only to fall into a deep sleep. While he's asleep, God reveals how his offspring will end up in slavery for 400 years but will be released from it with great wealth. Then, finally, Abram awakens to see a torch and a smoking pot floating through the symbols of death as God was making the covenant without him. The smoking pot and the torch are understood to have been God's way to reveal His presence as the One walking through the two halves because His presence is often related directly to fire in the Scriptures (see also Exod. 3:2; 13:21-22; 14:24; 19:18).

Abram's mortality left him unable to make the covenant with God since he would be long dead before the events of Exodus. So, God ensured the covenant would be kept by making it with Himself, causing Abram and his offspring to be beneficiaries of the covenant.

This example foreshadows how the great gospel covenant of the Cross would be made not *with* humanity but *for* humanity.[4]

How that plays out is revealed in Smith's other two examples.

REPRESENTED AND BENEFICIARIES

The second example is when David faced Goliath in 1 Samuel 17.[5]

For six weeks, the Philistine champion insulted the terrified Israelite army. Goliath brazenly challenged the children of Israel to present a champion. They would fight as representatives of their nations. The loser's nation would be enslaved to the victor's nation.

David arrives, sees what is happening, and asks Saul for permission to *represent* Israel, which he receives.

This is a vital key. In a covenant, there is a representative from each party. In essence, the people being represented are *in* their representative. In David's case, the entire nation of Israel was *in* David. Another word for this would be a *mediator*.

It must have been disconcerting for the armies of Israel to see this gangly teen going out into the field of battle with all their families and futures resting on his boney shoulders and sling.

The Lord ultimately gives David the victory. As he lifts Goliath's recently liberated head from his body, the army of Israel floods onto the battlefield, plundering the Philistines and shouting in victory.

Smith says that they were rejoicing in a victory where they brought nothing but several weeks of cowardice. But they celebrated because the victory also belonged to them since "they had been 'in' their representative and shared his victory as if it were their own." [6]

Ephesians 2:4-9

*But God, being rich in mercy, **because of the great love with which he loved us,** even when we were dead in our trespasses, made us alive together with Christ— by grace you have been saved—and raised us up with him and seated us with him in the heavenly places in Christ Jesus, so that in the coming ages he **might show the immeasurable riches of his grace in kindness toward us** in Christ Jesus. **For by grace you have been saved through faith. And this is not your own doing; it is the gift of God, not a result of works, so that no one may boast.***

The key for us to understand is that we brought nothing to this battle. Jesus, our representative, fought a battle on our behalf that we could have never won. Humanity was in Christ and therefore crucified with Him. He didn't just die for us, but as us.

Let me explain further: there is a direct convergence between Abram's covenant and the covenant of the Cross. God represented both parties for His promise with Abram. And He did the same for us.

God the Father, representing deity, and Jesus the Incarnate Son, representing humanity, made a covenant with each other, making humanity the beneficiaries of a better covenant. In this, God made a covenant with God and we benefit because we were in Christ!

Hebrews 8:6

*But as it is, Christ has **obtained a ministry that is as much more excellent** than the old as the **covenant he mediates is better**, since it is enacted on **better promises**.*

The gospel is often reduced to the statement, *Jesus died for you, so you should live for Him*. However, it results in a misunderstanding of this saving grace, potentially leading us into a religious mindset where we must work for our salvation. The Cross is a complete work, and it requires no help from us.

Ephesians 2:8-9

*For by grace you have been saved through faith. And this is not your own doing; **it is the gift of God, not a result of works**, so that no one may boast.*

Salvation isn't earned, it's given.

But just when we think this covenant couldn't get better, it does!

The last example we will look at from Smith's perspective is again from David's life, but now with his best friend Jonathan's son, Mephibosheth.[7]

Jonathan and David were best friends and loved each other with godly love. In 1 Samuel 20, they make a covenant between them to show kindness to each other's families forever. Soon after, Jonathan and his father, King Saul, lose their lives in battle, and the royal house of Israel falls into dread, hiding all of Jonathan's children to avoid being slaughtered by whoever ascends the throne of Israel. In a panic, a nurse carrying the toddler Mephibosheth drops him, and cripples him for the rest of his life.

David eventually takes the throne of Israel, which God had promised him, and in 2 Samuel 9, he remembers his covenant with Jonathan. So, he asks if anyone is left in Jonathan's household he can show kindness to.

David finds out there is a surviving son, Mephibosheth, who is in hiding in Lo Debar. So, David summons him to the throne room.

This would have been terrifying for Mephibosheth because he would have been taught the king would kill him. He would have been taught David was a rebel, a usurper, a murderer, and should never be trusted. Mephibosheth would have been told the monster, David, hated him and wanted to do him harm.

When Mephibosheth gets to the throne room, David's first words are to encourage Mephibosheth not to fear. He then declares that Mephibosheth would surely receive the same kindness David would have shown to Mephibosheth's father, Jonathan.

This is the point of the covenant. Mephibosheth discovered there was a promise working for him before he ever existed. And that David delighted in Mephibosheth in the same way he delighted in Jonathan.

In the same way, you and I were left crippled by our sinful condition. Hiding away and deceived, thinking an angry king was looking to end us for just being born into the wrong family.

But to our great relief, we discover that He wants to adopt us into His family, and He delights in us in the same way He delights in the one He made the covenant with on our behalf, Jesus!

God delights in you like He delights in Jesus; that, my friend, is good news!

The gospel is a covenant with God the Father representing deity and Jesus representing humanity, resulting in humanity as the beneficiary.

That is why we receive an inheritance and not a wage.

Ephesians 2:8-9
For *by grace you have been saved through faith*. And *this is not your own doing; it is the gift of God*, *not a result of works*, *so that no one may boast*.

There is an essential element regarding grace I want to establish at this early point in our journey together.

We tend to define grace from the perspective of our unconditional acceptance by God. While true, that's only a partial perspective that robs us of healthy understanding.

The word *charis* is the word for grace and is linked to joy. Grace and joy are connected. In its definition, *charis* is an attitude of joy toward someone. Grace is God's attitude of joy toward humanity.

Often grace gets incompletely defined and, frankly, understandably so, as unmerited favour. Except it *is* merited, not by us, but by Jesus. Grace is God's joyful view of man because of Jesus.

God delights in us because of Jesus.

2 Corinthians 1:20

*For **all the promises of God find their Yes in him.**
That is why it is **through him** that we utter **our amen**
to God for his glory.*

We engage grace at a whole new level, and it makes more sense when tethered to the gospel. The better our understanding of the gospel, the better our understanding of grace.

The next Chapter will examine how we will move forward in the *Gears of Grace.*

STUDY QUESTIONS

What is your definition of God's grace, and why?

Read Matthew 19:16-24 and Matthew 25:14-30. How is Jesus showing us that He is not driven by any ideology but by the agenda of His Father?

How has your understanding of the gospel changed in light of understanding it as a covenant?

What changes in you when you hear that God delights in you in the same way He delights in Jesus?

CHAPTER 2

SHIFTING GEARS

ONE DAY WHILE DRIVING, I WAS SHIFTING THROUGH THE GEARS of a standard transmission, getting up to highway speed. The Lord spoke to me when I put the car into fifth gear on the highway. He said, *"There are Gears of Grace that get you to destiny speed."*

Perplexed, I began praying and reading through Scripture to understand what the different Gears of Grace might be. Then, a sense of what God wanted me to discover came to light.

To understand the symbolism behind the Gears of Grace, it is essential to understand what it is like to shift gears in a standard vehicle.

In a five-speed vehicle, five gears are available for increasing desired speeds. Now I am not mechanically inclined, but for the sake of the revelation of this book, we need to have a basic understanding of what happens when we shift gears.

When you are accelerating in, let's say first gear, and come to the end of its capacity, you feel the tension in the vehicle because the engine is revving at its red-line. So, to address the tension, you release the accelerator and press on the clutch pedal, which separates the drive shaft from the engine, letting the flywheel rotate freely. Because of its momentum, the vehicle coasts for a moment. As it coasts, you manually shift the transmission into the next gear, and now engage the new gear's potential.

ACCELERATE – TENSION – CLUTCH – NEW GEAR

This is important because, for many of us in our journey with God, we live in tension and are unable to move beyond it, because we haven't learned to shift gears. And, so we try to accelerate but get frustrated feeling like God has more for us, but we're unable to gain speed no matter how hard we pray or perform. Here, so many get discouraged and just think, "Oh well, I guess this just isn't for me," or they slip into an offense with God feeling like He is letting them down, rather than shifting in new revelations of God's grace.

ACCELERATE!

You and I are made to grow. This is the acceleration: growing in the knowledge, relationship, and ways of God. Physically, the end of growth is the start of its decline. Spiritually, we are connected to an infinite God; therefore, our growth is meant to be eternal. Part of the joy of Heaven will be to discover our infinite Father for eternity.

So then, it stands to reason that our acceleration or growth is natural and expected as we move forward in our journey with God. As we relate to Him in a new way, that new way will accelerate us into something else that's new and powerful. This new level of speed will challenge old mindsets and behaviours and bring us into a new level of tension.

Romans 1:17

For in it the righteousness of God is revealed from faith to faith, as it is written, "The righteous shall live by faith."

2 Corinthians 3:17-18

*Now the Lord is the Spirit, and where the Spirit of the
Lord is, there is freedom. And we all, with unveiled
face, beholding the glory of the Lord, **are being transformed into the same image from one degree of glory
to another.***

Your life's lessons are to become the building blocks for others.
One encounter is the foundation for the next encounter. Your acceleration shouldn't be from a standstill, but rather from the momentum
created by the stewardship of the last thing God has revealed to you.

New revelation addresses that tension and removes the old way of
thinking to make space for a new heavenly way of thinking, giving us
access to accelerate once again.

THE TENSION – ADDRESSING TENSION

The first key is to face the tension full on. Often, believers try to
avoid tension because of the distasteful truth behind that tension.
Tension isn't a bad thing, nor is it a sign of God's frustration with you.
Always remember that God's joyful attention toward you is at the core
of grace. Instead of running from tension, learn from it. Let the tension
point you to the next level of freedom the Lord has for you. Physically,
our muscles develop by exposing them to tension through the strain of
weight resistance, and the result is growth. So many aspects of our lives
revolve around the principle of addressing tension. However, we often
avoid tension instead of facing it.

John Maxwell, a front-runner in leadership and leadership devel-
opment, often refers to what he calls leadership lids, which are areas
in any leader's methods or personality needing to grow because they
hinder the leader from accessing their potential.[8] Their willingness to
address these leadership lids determines whether they will advance as
leaders, remain where they are, or decline.

As a Pastor, there is nothing more disappointing for me than to sit across from someone I can see so much potential in, who is refusing to face tension and is denying the fullness of what God has for them. Instead of moving forward in Jesus, they choose to remain under the lid of their tension and never move beyond it. The epidemic of apathy in the Body of Christ, especially in North America, is robbing the world of seeing the gospel at full speed.

> *The epidemic of apathy in the Body of Christ, especially in North America, is robbing the world of seeing the gospel at full speed.*

We must face the tension head-on. Embrace the tension and grow.

TENSION'S KEY

At the root of tension in our journey is the desire to have four intrinsic questions answered.

Am I Accepted?

Am I Valued?

Am I Able?

Do I Matter?

These aren't questions answered through natural means. They are answered through the affirmation experienced and provided in God's love. I'm not speaking of the human expression of love, but of *agape* love expressed by our Father in Heaven. *Agape* love is the love expressed to humanity and experienced by us as individuals through the Cross. It's the love that motivated the covenant of the gospel. This love is revealed to us as unconditional and unearned, yet it is ours because God directs it toward us. It's a love not based on beauty but declares us beautiful, not on value but declares us valuable, and not in worthiness but declares we are worthy.

His Love, His Capacity

Often, human limitations are put on God's love because we tend to view Him through our limited lens of humanity, which means we project our natural limitations on God's capacity. So, for example, when it comes to grace, we project "If He is like me" perspectives of God's grace.

Let me explain.

Let's say you have a reasonably large capacity for grace and can extend favour to people without too much effort. But still, you encounter people that have run that tank dry and have pushed your capacity to its limit. The thought would be this, "Well, I have a pretty gracious heart, but if God is anything like me, He might possess more, but at some point, He is going to reach His limit!"

Here is the problem with that theology: *God has no limits. He is infinite! His grace is infinite, His patience...infinite, His love...infinite.* Every aspect of the nature/character of God is without limit. Every gift of the Spirit that He gives to us, He possesses in endless supply.

The enemy sows this trick into the hearts of Christians to make them think "If He is anything like me," in an attempt to conform God into the image of humans. However, through Jesus and the empowerment of the Holy Spirit, humans are meant to be conformed into the image of God!

So, when we speak of *agape* love, we are speaking of the love that reflects the infinite capacity of God. *Agape* love is expressed through us as Spirit-led and Spirit-filled believers. We don't have a capacity to receive or express *agape* love outside of our baptism into Christ and subsequent baptism in the Holy Spirit.

Jesus revealed this to us with his encounter with Peter in restoring their relationship after Peter denied Jesus before the Cross.

> *John 21:15-17*
>
> *When they had finished breakfast, Jesus said to Simon Peter, "Simon, son of John, **do you love me more than these?**" He said to him, "Yes, Lord; **you know that I love you.**" He said to him, "Feed my lambs." He said to him a second time, "Simon, son of John, **do you love me?**" He said to him, "Yes, Lord; **you know that I love you.**" He said to him, "Tend my sheep." He said to him the third time, "Simon, son of John, **do you love me?**" **Peter was grieved because he said to him the third time, "Do you love me?"** and he said to him, "Lord, you know everything; you know that I love you."* Jesus said to him, "Feed my sheep.*

This beautiful encounter has so many powerful truths, and there's a lovely message for us to understand *agape* love versus our human equivalents. But to truly gain the moment's impact, we must visit Peter's conversation with Jesus just a few days prior.

> *Matthew 26:31-35*
>
> *Then Jesus said to them, "You will all fall away because of Me this night. For it is written, 'I will strike the Shepherd, and the sheep of the flock will be scattered.' But after I am raised up, I will go before you to Galilee." Peter answered Him, "**though they all fall away because of you, I will never fall away.**" Jesus said to him, "Truly, I tell you, this very night, before the rooster crows, you will deny me three times." **Peter said to him, "Even if I must die with you, I will not deny you!"** And all the disciples said the same.*

Later that night, Peter denied Jesus and had his first real identity crisis, which Jesus would disarm through His love.

This love conversation on the beach is Peter's first conversation with Jesus after his denial. The air must have been tense, as all are likely wondering what would transpire. Will Jesus rebuke Peter? He did deserve it. Would he belittle Peter? Perhaps punish him?

Instead, we are given a glimpse into the wonderful nature of the *agape* love of God.

In their exchange, they use different words for love. They use the words *agape* and *phileo*. *Agape*, as mentioned earlier, is the God-like love expressed first to us through the Cross and then through us because of the Cross. *Phileo* love is brotherly affection.

Jesus asks Peter, "Do you love (*agape*) me?" Peter responds by saying, "You know that I love (*phileo*) you." After asking the question in the same manner the second time, with the same response from Peter for His third question, Jesus changes tactics. He asks, "Peter, do you love (*phileo*) me?" Peter answers, "Lord, you know everything. You know that I love (*phileo*) you."

In His first two questions, Jesus asked if Peter had God-love for Jesus. Peter answered by saying he realized that he had brotherly affection for Jesus. [9]

Jesus was bringing Peter face to face with the limits of his humanity for two reasons. The first reason is so that Peter would have a revelation that within himself, he was always going to fall short of the love that God possessed for him. Therefore, no form of human acceptance, praise, strength, or value would compare to those God gave us.

The hint towards the second reason hides in plain sight in Luke 24:49.

Luke 24:49

"And behold, I am sending the promise of my Father upon you. But stay in the city until you are clothed with power from on high."

Jesus was referring to the upcoming baptism in the Holy Spirit that would link humanity to the infinite nature of the Trinity.

In this incredible exchange with Peter, Jesus disarms the lie that human capacity could ever compare to God's. It was like Jesus said to Peter, "Do you see how you can't, but I can?"

Consider that today about your perspective. Can you see how you can't, but He can?

Proverbs 13:12

Hope deferred makes the heart sick, but a desire fulfilled is a tree of life.

We have desires hard-wired into our psyche. As mention earlier, they result in four fundamental questions that may be answered along many pathways, some of which can lead to profound bondage and pain. But to attain the outcome of the healthiest version of ourselves, we find the answers in connection with God's love through His grace.

FOUR FUNDAMENTAL QUESTIONS ABOUT DESIRES

Am I Accepted?

The answers to the inner longings for belonging, security, stability, worthiness, and inner peace are in this question of acceptance. Knowing that you are entirely accepted through God's love for you is the most liberating and robust foundation for the first three Gears of Grace.

Am I Valued?

The urgency of our heart's cry for value is steeped in our desire to know that we belong because of lineage, ancestry, and connection. Not valued for what we do or bring, but for who we are. We would still be loved and wanted because we simply exist, even if we did nothing else. This powerful question is answered continuously in the Gears of Grace.

Am I Able?

"You can do it!" are words every human needs to hear. Not just elementary praise that encourages you to try, which is essential and answered in being accepted and valued; but the clear statement of belief in our capacity. That encouragement breeds the confidence to take risks as we move forward in the Gears of Grace.

Do I Matter?

What is the mark that I am leaving on humanity? Do I have a purpose or a reason for breathing? Credit goes to Mark Twain for saying that the two most important days of our lives are when we are born and when we discover why. The why of our lives is most elusive because we try to answer it through what we do, what we acquire, who we have power over, and our position of importance.

FULFILLED THROUGH INTIMACY

The answers to these fundamental questions will determine whether the mark we leave will have a powerful or pitiful effect on those around us. We brilliantly experience our purpose as we journey through the Gears of Grace.

The desire to have these questions answered is good, and God wants your desires fulfilled.

John 16:23-24

*In that day, you will ask nothing of me. Truly, truly, I say to you, **whatever you ask of the Father in my name, he will give it to you.** Until now, you have asked nothing in my name. Ask, and you will receive that your joy may be full.*

Unfortunately, many get deceived by the enemy to have these questions answered through unhealthy or sinful ways. "Do I Matter?" is a good and healthy question rooted in the desire to have an impact. But if that "mattering" leads us to self-indulgent power-seeking, we have looked to have meaning outside of what God provides and have fallen victim to the enemy's lies of satiation versus satisfaction. Those lies lead us to satiate desires rather than satisfy them. One is attached to a craving, but the other is to fulfilment.

Desires are good. However, they need to be submitted to the Lordship of Jesus, for example. Vitamin C is good for me. But if Vitamin C were all I ate, it would become toxic. So too, desires not submitted to the Lordship of Jesus are at risk of becoming toxic, resulting in a poisoned person. Jesus has provided pathways for our desires to be fulfilled. Going outside those pathways results in a selfish addiction to sin for the satisfaction of our desires, leading us to become stunted and self-centred.

However, in the question of 'Do I Matter?' the one who learns to receive the recognition of Jesus will not be subject to the collateral attack of the enemy because they are finding their recognition hidden in Christ. And in that hiddenness, they are safe and at peace.

The fantastic part of these God-given questions is that they become our unique way of intimately connecting with Jesus. In other words, through the four fundamental questions, He has hard-wired into each of us an intensely personal and original way of experiencing intimacy with Him. This intimacy is entirely our own and no one else's. This means that your intimate relationship with Jesus is distinctly yours and yours alone.

THE DANGER OF COMPARISON

Unfortunately, a pitfall many believers fall into is comparison. In our social media, pop-culture world, we consistently compare our lives to the latest post from someone else's apparently perfect life. Unfortunately, the spirit of comparison's assignment is to measure us against a lie, and as a result, we feel like we will never measure up.

We do it in the church too. We compare our relationship with Jesus by what we perceive to be another's healthier or more vibrant relationship with Jesus. Since we feel we will never attain another's apparent experience with God, we are left discouraged and frustrated and tend to give up. And we stop our own personal pursuit of God because it probably won't ever be as good as what we see on another's social media feed.

Your relationship with Jesus isn't supposed to look like someone else's. The spirit of religion's assignment is to make everyone look the same, but Jesus wants an exclusive and individual relationship with you. He is not interested in having the same relationship with two different people.

I once heard it said that the creative nature of God couldn't be satisfied through copying. Because of that, when we try to copy the experience or anointing of another person, one of us becomes irrelevant.

We disarm comparison when we understand our unique way of connecting with Jesus through our own God-given answers. We can have full intimacy with God, custom-made for us as individuals.

What an incredible truth! This wonderful, infinite God created me with my own powerful and exclusive form of intimacy with Him.

> *When we experience a disillusion about God, it is because we have believed an illusion about God.*

Proving to me again, He loves me just as He created me to be *and* wants me to be me.

Throughout the rest of the book, I will be identifying the broad heading that the tension will be under, and you'll have to do the heavy lifting and allow the Holy Spirit to show you what tension you're dealing with and the desire that you are trying to fulfill outside of Jesus.

TENSION IS A GIFT

It is important to share another point about tension, and we will see this at work in later gears that have us moving near or at destiny speed. Whether the result of facing sinful patterns or mindsets that are deficient and rob us from experiencing more of God, tension is a gift.

To face tension with integrity requires honesty with God about the tension. God isn't intimidated by our sins, nor is He afraid of our questions. He isn't insecure and unable to hear our disappointments or where we feel disillusioned. A dear friend of mine, who walks in beautiful intimacy with Jesus, shared this powerful thought.

When we experience experience a disillusion about God, it is because we have believed an illusion about God.

Our tension can bring us to the point of true openness and transparency with God. That openness and transparency is actually the place to start experiencing new intimacy with God. Honesty about our sin, pain, disappointment, disillusionment, or confusion, opens the door for true inner healing through an encounter with Jesus. Or, for our metaphor of shifting through the gears of grace, the Clutch.

THE CLUTCH

The tension at the end of a gear feels like a glass ceiling. We know that God has more for us, but we can't seem to break through on our own. The way to relieve the tension felt in a vehicle when driving is to disengage the engine from the driveshaft using the clutch. The momentum created by the speed limit of the current gear allows for the vehicle to coast for a moment. In a sense, for it to rest, causing a *moment in its momentum,* creating the opportunity to shift gears. So we shift into the next gear and release the clutch while simultaneously stepping on the accelerator.

A MOMENT IN OUR MOMENTUM

Similarly, when we feel tension in our lives and are desiring more in our walk with Jesus but are seemingly unable to break through, we need to pause and quiet down to engage the clutch, and hear from the Holy Spirit for His guidance.

This is the *moment in our momentum,* a *rest encounter,* where our honesty with Jesus opens doors for the next gear we are shifting to.

There are two biblical principles attached to this *rest encounter* with Jesus. The first is in the Gospel of Luke where a blind man is calling out to Jesus.

> *Luke 18:38-43 (ESV)*
> **And he cried out, "Jesus, Son of David, have mercy on me!" And those who were in front rebuked him, telling him to be silent. But he cried out all the more, "Son of David, have mercy on me!" And Jesus stopped and commanded him to be brought to him. And when he came near, he asked him, "What do you want me to do for you?" He said, "Lord, let me recover my sight." And Jesus said to him, "Recover**

your sight; your faith has made you well." And im-
mediately he recovered his sight and followed him,
glorifying God. And all the people, when they saw it,
gave praise to God.

It seems odd that Jesus would lack the discernment to see what the man wanted. But Jesus asked the blind man what he wanted Him to do. The man asks to see and is healed.

In the *moment in our momentum*, we have permission to ask what we want from Jesus. Especially if it seems obvious, because sometimes *why* we come to Him isn't *what* we leave with. This leads to the second principle of the *rest encounter,* found in John 4:1-30.

John writes that Jesus is sitting at the well when the Samaritan woman comes to draw water and He asks her for a drink. In this powerful conversation between them, Jesus reveals Himself as the living water, and if she drinks of His water, she'd never thirst again. Upon asking for the water, Jesus invites her to go and get her husband and come back. She replies that she has no husband and Jesus agrees.

John 4:17-18 (ESV) 17
The woman answered him, "I have no husband."
Jesus said to her, "You are right in saying, 'I have no
husband'; 18 for you have had five husbands, and the
*one you now have is not your husband. **What you have***
said is true."

In the *moment in our momentum*, Jesus will also reveal where we have been walking in partial truths, and He will bring light to those areas so that we can be whole in Him.

She came to draw water, but after her encounter with Jesus, she left her water jar and went on to tell people of her meeting Jesus. Eastern Orthodox tradition reveals her as St. Photini, the first evangelist, and was considered equal to the apostles. A powerful woman, who was martyred for confronting the Roman emperor Nero with the gospel.

She came desiring water, and left with a destiny.

Timing, Timing, Timing...

I once heard John Maxwell say that the difference between a home run and a foul ball is timing. A powerful statement indeed. In our example of shifting gears, timing is very important as well. If you don't embrace the moment in the momentum, you will try to jam yourself into the next gear of grace and end up grinding the gears, or said another way, religiously work your way into the next gear.

At the same time, should you ride the clutch too long, you will lose the momentum provided by the gear you were in and find that you need to stay in the former gear.

But if you honour the moment in the momentum and respond to where Jesus wants to bring wholeness, you will shift into the next gear.

So how do we shift into the new gear from this place of rest? There are three stages that we will discuss in each Chapter for the steward-ship of the clutch. Repent, Renew, and Respond.

Repent

> *Hebrews 6:1*
> *Therefore, let us leave the **elementary doctrine of Christ** and go on to maturity, not laying again a foundation of **repentance from dead works** and of faith toward God.*

The writer of Hebrews starts Chapter six by encouraging readers to move out of the elementary doctrines and toward maturity. The first one is repentance from dead works.

BRAKES AND PAVEMENT –
UNDERSTANDING REPENTANCE

Repentance is a word that is often used in discipleship; however, it is not entirely understood.

When I was eleven-years old, my parents started to give me a weekly allowance, and I decided to use it to purchase a new bike.

I had a red five-speed at the time but was outgrowing it, and I needed a new bike. But not just any bike, a ten-speed bike. So, I began to save. I saved for most of the year to buy my new ten-speed.

We lived in a small town, so we had to travel to another larger community to shop at a sporting goods store and purchased my new ride there. It was a sleek, black ten-speed with chrome on the pedals, and it was amazing! And soon enough, it was mine.

I'll never forget the day we brought my new bike home. I was so excited to show it off to my friends. My dad helped me unload it from the back of our pickup, and then he grinned at me and said, "Go show it off, son!" So, I hopped onto my new bike and took off.

My friends lived only a few blocks away and would be playing street hockey in their driveway, so I had to work hard to get through all the gears to go top speed in tenth gear by the time I reached their house.

My old bike was ok, but it only had five gears, and the back brakes didn't work, so all I ever used were the front brakes, which were worn down and took a long time to stop my bike.

So, there I was, peddling as fast as I could in tenth gear, likely breaking the sound barrier when flying up to my friend's home. Out of habit, I tried to stop with the front brakes, which, unlike my old bike, grabbed instantly; I remember this part as if it were in slow motion. Slowly, I felt the back wheel of my new ten-speed rise as I was pitched forward because of my momentum propelling me over top of the handlebars.

At this point, I had a sickening realization that I was going in the wrong direction. The pavement would ultimately confirm what I had come to discern.

Repentance is the sickening realization that we are going in the wrong direction. But the beauty of repentance is we don't need to meet the pavement, but we can course correct mid-air!

The first step to getting ready to shift gears is repentance, or changing our mind about our direction and how we are trying to fulfill that desire.

You may say, "I don't know what the tension is, what the desire is, or what I need to repent from."

I have good news. Your task isn't to be the one identifying what needs addressing. Instead, the Holy Spirit is responsible for revealing it to you.

> *John 16:8-11*
> *And when he comes, he will **convict the world** **concerning sin and righteousness and judgment:** concerning sin, because they do not believe in me; concerning righteousness, because I go to the Father, and you will see me no longer; concerning judgment, because the ruler of this world is judged.*

The Holy Spirit oversees clarifying what isn't righteous to the believer. In asking the Holy Spirit to speak to you about these things and to reveal what needs addressing to relieve the tension, you are forging intimacy with God. What an amazing gift!

Intimacy is the outcome of your pursuit of the Lord and your invitation to the Holy Spirit to search your heart, reveal your desires, and how you've wrongly fulfilled those desires.

RENEWAL

> *Hebrews 6:1*
> *Therefore, let us leave the **elementary doctrine of Christ** and go on to maturity, not laying again a foundation of repentance from dead works and of faith toward God.*

A mistake often made when we repent is changing our mind, but not renewing it.

People tell me they have repented of an issue over and over again but still struggle with that issue. Often the reason is while they may have repented, they aren't bearing the fruit of repentance.

> *Matthew 3:7-8*
> *But when he saw many of the Pharisees and Sadducees coming to his baptism, he said to them, "You brood of vipers! Who warned you to flee from the wrath to come? **Bear fruit in keeping with repentance.**"*

John the Baptist challenges the religious order of the day, to not only pay lip service to repentance, but to actually engage repentance and bear its fruit.

Dr. Randy Clark describes the process as going in one direction, then realizing it's the wrong direction and changing our mind about going in that direction. That is repentance. But to turn and go in a different direction is the fruit of repentance.

So, repentance is incomplete if we decide to turn *from* something without turning *to* something: we turn to God and his ways. This is where faith toward God comes into play.

> *Romans 12:1-2*
>
> *I appeal to you therefore, brothers, by the mercies of God, to present your bodies as a living sacrifice, holy and acceptable to God, which is your spiritual worship. Do **not be conformed** to this world, but **be transformed** by the **renewal of your mind,** that by testing you may discern what is the will of God, what is good and acceptable and perfect.*

In my book, *Renovated for Glory,* I break down the renewal of the mind at length. For our journey together, I will simply say that the renewal of the mind is learning what Heaven thinks on a subject and making that my truth.

There is a connection between the fruit of repentance and the elementary doctrine of faith toward God found in Hebrews 6.

If we turn away from temptation but don't turn toward something else, we will return to the thing satiating that temptation in the first place. There is a misconception that repentance removes temptation. It doesn't. But it provides a pathway for a deeper walk with God when we invite the Holy Spirit to show us what Heaven says about the desire behind the temptation. When we don't learn what Heaven thinks about fulfilling that desire, the temptation to return to the former dysfunctional way leaves us in our tension. However, when we learn Heaven's thoughts on our desires, we engage a pathway toward freedom.

RESPOND

Once we have learned what Heaven thinks, we need to act.

James 4:17
**So whoever knows the right thing to do and fails to
do it, for him, it is sin.**

During one of my first driving lessons with my dad, he told me
to change lanes. I checked my mirrors, then signalled and started to
change lanes. Then, he startled me by firmly telling me to stop because
I would hit someone.

I obeyed him but told him I had checked all my mirrors and no
one was there. So, he told me to look over my left shoulder, and to my
shock, I saw a big pickup truck in the lane beside me. That's when I
learned that the mirrors don't tell the whole story and that there is a
blind spot requiring a shoulder check.

Now that first blunder didn't make me a bad driver. However, if
I had learned about the blind spot and continued to drive, aware of it
but not changing my driving habits, I would be a bad driver. But ever
since I learned of the blind spot, I've been aware of it. In other words, I
responded to what I learned.

It is not enough to turn from something and learn what Heaven
thinks about it to alleviate the tension. Instead, we must respond to
what we have learned and live out of our new understanding.

Let me give you an example. Say a person's desire is security. So,
to manage security, they respond by being stingy with their finances
and unwilling to be generous. Then, in their tension, the Holy Spirit
reveals that the most powerful way to remain secure is to be generous
with finances. So, they repent after learning what Heaven thinks about
their security, but remain stingy and avoid generosity.

What do you think will happen? Their tension will remain because
they are not responding to what they've learned.

James 1:22-24

*But **be doers of the word**, and not hearers only, deceiving yourselves. For if anyone is a hearer of the word and not a doer, he is like a man who looks intently at his natural face in a mirror. For he looks at himself and **goes away** and at once **forgets what he was like**.*

This is the challenge that so often gets left undone. To actually engage in change is the key to growing in God. This book doesn't bring some sort of silver bullet to the disciple's life to ensure growth without cost.

Change is the necessary ingredient for our growth.

THE NEW GEAR

Responding is what brings us into the next gear. Causing us to overcome the tension, allowing for new acceleration in our growth, and moving us closer to destiny speed.

Philippians 3:13-16

*Brothers, I do not consider that I have made it my own. But one thing I do: **forgetting what lies behind** and **straining forward to what lies ahead, I press on** toward the goal for **the prize of the upward call of God** in Christ Jesus. Let those of **us who are mature think this way**, and if in anything **you think otherwise**, God will **reveal that also to you**. Only let us hold true to what we have attained.*

START YOUR ENGINES...

Before we begin, let's discuss two essential elements. The first is the unique way the gears are divided because there are two levels of discipleship. Those levels manifest themselves in the natural break between the third and fourth gears, in the same way that you can begin to hit highway speeds at the apex of the third gear going into the fourth.

For the sake of being able to reference them, I will share the first level of discipleship with you.

Philippians 2:9-11
Therefore, God has highly exalted Him and bestowed on Him the **Name that is above every name,** so that **at the Name of Jesus** every knee should bow, in Heaven and on earth and under the earth, and every tongue confess **that Jesus Christ is Lord,** to the glory of God the Father.

Over the years, I struggled to try to define discipleship. Then, a few years back, I worked hard to engage a healthy definition and stumbled upon a thought from Alan Hirsch in his book *The Forgotten Ways.* Hirsch defines discipleship by starting with this understanding: Jesus is Lord.[10] He called it three words that are a worldview. I love that thought. Looking at life through the lens of "Jesus is Lord."

So, as I fought for a healthy definition, I landed on this; discipleship is deliberate submission to the Lordship of Jesus. Said another way, it is choosing to submit my ways to His ways. To activate the thought, the Lord put this phrase in my heart. Permission, not presumption. In other words, don't presume to act without the consent of Jesus.

I go into greater detail about the two levels of discipleship in my book *Renovated for Glory,* but these definitions hold great value for our understanding of grace.

While this definition of discipleship proved helpful, it was also birthed somewhat from a religious mindset. Therefore, as God's grace became more evident, I needed to add a second definition for discipleship, which I will share between the third and fourth gears.

In this first level of discipleship, Jesus is Lord, and permission, not presumption, are essential to moving through the first three Gears of Grace.

GOD THE GARDENER

Secondly, there are two different forms of encounters with God. One manifests in the first three gears and the second in the last three. So, in the first three gears, there are three gardens that we have to visit.

Genesis 2:8
*And the **Lord God** planted a garden in Eden, in the east, and there he put the man whom he had formed.*

Genesis 2:15
*The Lord God **took the man and put him in the garden** of Eden **to work it and keep it.***

The word "planted" also means established. God established our gardens through the Cross.

We could never accomplish the work completed through the life of Jesus and His sacrifice on the Cross. But God places us in these gardens to work them and keep them. This means we are responsible for growing and engaging the challenges we face. Rather than trying to run from them, we should run to them.

There has been an alarming trend in the Body of Christ to want a silver bullet in the form of a prayer, deliverance, or through some form of impartation, to just have everything be magically better. And while God, from time to time, does miraculously set people free from things, more often than not, He partners with us to teach us how to be victors, overcoming every attack of the enemy.

Romans 8:37
*No, in all these things **we are more than conquerors
through him** who loved us.*

I will share another form of an encounter between third and fourth gear when we arrive there.

Let's continue journeying toward maturity through the Gears of Grace.

STUDY QUESTIONS

Look over the list of questions. Then, take a moment and ask Jesus how you have been trying to answer those questions outside of His provision.

Am I Accepted?

Am I Valued?

Am I Able?

Do I Matter?

In what ways could your answers become pathways to greater intimacy with Jesus?

How have you allowed comparing your faith journey to others to affect your pursuit of God?

Can you see areas where you have repented but haven't pursued the renewal of your mind? Ask God how He wants you to think about those areas, and what would be one positive response that you could implement?

CHAPTER 3

FIRST GEAR: GOD'S DELIGHT IN EXTENDING MERCY

THE GUARANTEE OF FORGIVENESS

Hebrews 4:16
Let us then, with confidence, draw near to the throne
of grace that we may receive mercy and find grace to
help in time of need.

IN THE TOWN I GREW UP IN, WE HAD A DENTIST WHO WAS QUITE wealthy. Every year, he would purchase a new Volvo. They were generally gold, four-door sedans he would drive to and from his office. They also had manual transmissions.

I don't know why he would buy these beautiful cars with manual transmissions since he struggled with the whole concept of switching gears. But, morning and evening, you could hear his car screaming down the road as if the engine was begging him to shift out of first gear.

But it's a Lamborghini!

2 Corinthians 6:1
*Working together with him, then, we appeal to you **not** to receive the grace of God in vain.*

Imagine you had the opportunity to purchase a high-end sports car like a Lamborghini. You would go to a very exclusive car dealership and likely be treated like royalty considering the incredible cost of the vehicle.

As you look around the showroom, a salesperson comes up to you and starts to explain the car's features. Then he discusses with you the heart of the vehicle, the car's powerful engine. But in his explanation of the car's speed, he tells you its maximum speed is just under 50 kilometres per hour (30 MPH).

You would rightfully question the salesperson's knowledge of the car if he didn't know that it had more potential for speed than just the speed of its first gear.

Often teachers of grace are guilty of this same mistake, which is to reduce this infinite attribute of God, His grace, to its first gear.

Make no mistake, this gear is vital. There is no starting this journey without this gear. The car will not move without being in first gear. I don't want us to think this gear isn't essential; it is. But we must understand it isn't the only gear. God has more!

God's Delight to Extend Mercy

God's delight in extending mercy to His children is the first gear of grace. Remember, we learned the connection between grace and joy in the first Chapter, and that grace is an expression of God's attitude of joy toward us. To fully understand the power of the love of God made known in this gear, we need to return to the covenant.

Many Christians live in fear of sin separating them from God, which is a ploy of the enemy to establish a religious mindset. That mindset sets the stage for a legislative form of Christianity that loses its relational and love qualities, reducing what was meant to be a loving relationship founded in covenant, to a contractual exchange of goods and services. You live like a little soldier, and then you can come to Heaven.

There is a reason, however, that this is the first gear of grace. Mishandling this revelation of grace allows us to consider the tolerance of sin in our lives as appropriate. Remember the example of ditches being on either side of this road? The ultra-religious or ultra-permissive ditches both lack a healthy understanding of who God is.

Or, we can live in the radical centre that celebrates the righteous condition of holiness that is radically set apart as a result of grace, but living so freely that we can rejoice in the security of God's love if the lure of sin catches us.

UNDERSTANDING THE GEAR

Hebrews 9:24-28

*For Christ has entered, **not into holy places made with hands, which are copies of the true things,** but into Heaven itself, now to **appear in the presence of God on our behalf. Nor was it to offer himself repeatedly,** as the high priest enters the holy places every year with blood not his own, **for then He would have had to suffer repeatedly since the foundation of the world.** But as it is, **He has appeared once and for all** at the end of the ages to **put away sin by the sacrifice of Himself.** And just as it is appointed for man to die once, and after that comes judgment, so **Christ, having been offered once to bear the sins of***

many, will appear a second time, not to deal with sin
but to save those who are eagerly waiting for Him.

In understanding this first gear, we have to come to grips with an important revelation due to the covenant of the Cross. Sin isn't *being* dealt with on the Cross; it *has been* dealt with on the Cross. Or said another way, our sin is not *being* forgiven; it *was forgiven*, once and for all. This is one reason why the covenant of the Cross is so miraculous. Jesus died once and for all. Once, and for all of us. Once, and for all time. Once, and for all sin. Period.

We need not ever approach His throne fearfully. On the contrary, this work of the Cross guarantees us God's favour, just like David delighted in Mephibosheth; the King delights in us in the same way He delights in Jesus.

Hebrews 4:16
*Let us then, **with confidence,** draw near to the **throne** **of grace** that **we may receive mercy and find grace to** **help in time of need.***

The key is clarifying how this all works on our behalf. Hebrews 4:16 shows how grace and mercy work hand in hand for us.

Grace is God's joyful attitude toward us, and mercy is His response to our distress. Therefore, the word *eleos* which we translate as mercy, is an attitude of pity with the desire to resource the one in distress.

> Sin isn't *being* dealt with on the Cross; it *has been* dealt with on the Cross.

Vines Expository Dictionary uses this explanation.

"Mercy is the act of God; peace is the resulting experience in the heart of man. Grace describes God's attitude toward the lawbreaker and the rebel; mercy is His attitude toward those who are in distress."[11]

I will break down this thought in more depth in the next Chapter, but for our understanding of this first Gear of Grace, we need to open our eyes to what is happening.

Let me paraphrase Hebrews 4:16 this way;

Let us then confidently and with assurance come before the throne of His joyful attitude towards us so we can receive pity and power through joy, experiencing total forgiveness in our time of need.

1 John 1:9
If we confess our sins, He is faithful and just to forgive us our sins and to cleanse us from all unrighteousness.

Chuck Swindoll once wrote that if you aren't teaching grace in a way that could be misused, you aren't teaching grace.[12]

This gear is abused over and over again because it can be. While it could seem like God is being taken advantage of or even taken for a fool, He is not, nor is He unaware of the character flaw in any of His children mishandling this mighty gift.

For some, this may feel like an injustice. A disciple sinning whenever and wherever they want without any response from God except love? The short answer is "Yes," and the long answer is, "Yes ... but."

"Yes."

As just mentioned, the short answer to the promise of this first gear is "Yes."

2 Corinthians 1:20
*For **all the promises of God** find their yes **in Him**.*
That is why it is through Him that we utter our Amen
to God for His glory.

The promise of grace and mercy find their forever "Yes," in Jesus. As I shared earlier, the Cross isn't forgiving sin. It has forgiven sin. The covenant is done, and the unbreakable promise is activated in this first gear because of unconditional love. It is now the covenant right of any who confess Jesus as Lord to receive mercy and forgiveness.

As I mentioned when we discussed spiritual nearsightedness, we struggle with this covenant living because we are trying to view the infinite through a finite lens. There is no such thing as waste to the infinite because there is a never-ending supply. If we presume God has some limitations to His nature, eventually, we will presume there will be limitations on His attitude towards us.

A GOD LIKE ME

Here is how this gear is powerfully affected by spiritual nearsightedness, and I touched on this earlier but would like to break it down more now.

I am a gracious person. I generally have an open heart and can extend grace to people. Some would call it a large "grace tank." For whatever reason, I have a large capacity to be gracious to people. However, there are people on this planet Earth who have depleted my grace tank. In other words, they have exhausted my capacity for grace. Their presence grates on my emotions and patience like fingernails scraped across a chalkboard.

This isn't an indictment of my walk with God or people, but rather it's an example of how I have made the mistake of thinking that God is like me.

The big mistake in our understanding of the nature and makeup of God is we have adopted a superhuman perspective of God. We're tricked into thinking He is a super version of us as humans, as if God is just a perfect version of humanity.

"IF HE'S ANYTHING LIKE ME"

So, if I am gracious but can run out of it for some people, God, *if He is anything like me*, probably has quite a bit more grace than me, but I am sure, *like me*, He can run out of it at some point. And I have probably reached that point with Him. So, at some time, God will be sick of forgiving the same sin over and over again, and His grace will run out.

The great perversion of truth is that God is somehow conformed into the image of man. But the complete truth is man is meant to be conformed into the image of Jesus.

Not true.

Numbers 23:19

God is not man, that he should lie,
or a son of man, that he should change his mind.
Has he said, and will he not do it?
Or has he spoken, and will he not fulfill it?

The great news I have for you is that God is not a man in any way. He is not of the flesh, nor is He limited by emotions subject to circumstance, and He has never been or ever will be afraid.

The great perversion of truth is that God is somehow conformed into the image of man. But the complete truth is man is meant to be conformed into the image of Jesus.

1 Corinthians 15:49

*Just as we have **borne the image of the man of dust**,*
*we shall **also bear the image of the Man of Heaven**.*

Therefore, God is in no way limited in His grace. Since He is infinite, and He is love, His love, therefore, is infinite. Grace and mercy are expressions of His love.

Thus, God can give with no strings attached. It's why He can heal without someone choosing to follow Him. It's why He can love without people loving Him back. There is no thought as to His love, power, or grace as wasted on someone who hasn't responded well. He is a limitless supply and, therefore, able to liberally give and lavishly love and completely forgive without any risk of regret. Why? Because our God has never been, nor will He ever be, in lack. He has no savings account, for He will never need it.

His infinite nature is too great to ever understand, so we must accept it by faith.

Romans 8:1-2

*There is therefore now **no condemnation** for those who are **in Christ Jesus**. For the law of the Spirit of life **has set you free in Christ Jesus** from the law of sin and death.*

What an incredible gear this is! We can never be condemned if we choose to be in Christ. It is as if God is saying, "You are in Christ, and there is no punishment for Him. Therefore, there is no punishment for you!"

LET'S BE CLEAR

I want to be clear on one point in sharing this with you. I am not advocating that living in the first gear of grace alone is a sign of complete maturity. It saddens me to think some would say they have chosen to be a disciple but have not in any way reflected the Lordship of Jesus over their lives.

God is not a fool, but He is not a promise-breaker either. This Gear of Grace is the witness of His covenant-keeping nature.

2 Timothy 2:13

*If we are faithless, **He remains faithful**— for He cannot deny Himself.*

However, this doesn't result in a once-saved, always-saved mindset. I disagree with a doctrine that reduces the high price of the Cross to a simple little religious prayer with no reflection of engaging the life of the Kingdom behind it. If a person's life doesn't reflect their confession, doesn't the world have a right to question the validity of their confession? I am convinced that believers can allow themselves to be so deceived by sinfulness that they could consciously turn their back on their salvation.

But I think our salvation and God's joyful attitude towards us are harder to lose than the spirit of religion would like us to believe.

"Yes...but."

So, the answer remains yes, but there is a result in living in what we could call a permissive grace. And the result is this. You stay in first gear. Sinning and simply asking for forgiveness with no intention of embracing true life in Christ may not rob you of going to Heaven, but it will rob you of being rewarded by Heaven, and will most certainly rob the world of Heaven being experienced through you.

You cannot travel at the speed of destiny in first gear. And lack of progress comes as the result of choosing to live in first gear.

The Tension – Sin

Romans 6:15-16

What then? Are we to sin because we are not under law but under grace? By no means! Do you not know that if you present yourselves to anyone as obedient slaves, you are slaves of the one whom you obey, either of sin, which leads to death, or of obedience, which leads to righteousness?

The presence of sin in our lives causes the tension of this gear. I am not talking about the occasional slip into sinful behaviour, but rather a conscious choice to keep sin in our lives. I will not name things here because that's the Holy Spirit's role, but I will say if something is coming to mind right now, there is a very good chance the Holy Spirit is revealing the sin to you.

This isn't a "to sin or not to sin" issue; that is for a later gear. This tension is simply choosing to sin as a lifestyle because that behaviour is more attractive than discipleship. It's hanging on to sin as normal living. Is it possible to live sinfully and be unaware of it? Yes, which is why our relationship with the Holy Spirit holds such value.

> *This tension is simply choosing to sin as a lifestyle because that behaviour is more attractive than discipleship.*

According to what Paul wrote in Romans 6, to present ourselves to sin is to be enslaved. I think too often, believers don't realize the authority they possess. The fact is, we have so much authority that we will only be in bondage where we choose to be in bondage.

These strongholds are always demonic, but it doesn't always mean there is a need for some form of deliverance. Strongholds depend on individuals believing in and agreeing with a lie to form a thought pattern. My friend, Dr. Kim Maas, would say that sometimes it's a demon, but sometimes it's just your flesh, and you're unwilling to bring it into submission.

The first level of discipleship is manifest here. Is Jesus really Lord over these areas, or are we choosing lordship and making choices contrary to the Kingdom we represent? Yes, there is grace for forgiveness; this gear holds that promise. But the speed of destiny will remain out of range as long as slavery to sin remains our choice.

Modified behaviour isn't the pathway to transformation; it is the result of it.

God is not interested in the modification of behaviour. He wants the transformation of our lives by being conformed to the image of Jesus. Modified behaviour isn't the pathway to transformation; it is the result of it.

THE CLUTCH – SUBMISSION

James 4:7
Submit *yourselves, therefore to God.* **Resist the Devil,** *and he will flee from you.*

Submission is the clutch of this first gear for two reasons. First, scripturally, we need to submit ourselves to God to resist the Devil in the context of the temptation to sin. Second, submission plays a role in releasing the tension in every gear.

In this first gear, the goal is to establish submission to the Lordship of Jesus as a core value in our makeup. The clutch of submission in the first gear is not about overcoming a particular sin, but our posture towards the Lord so that we will live for Him.

The Gardens

As I shared earlier, the first three Gears of Grace have corresponding gardens we tend as disciples. In Genesis 2:15, God put Adam in the garden He had planted and told Adam to "work it and keep it." In our lives, we have three gardens to work and keep as we grow in God.

So then, what does this look like? What does submission to God look like, and how do we put submission into practice?

The Garden Tomb

> *John 19:41*
> *Now in the place where he was crucified there was a garden, and in the garden a new tomb in which no one had yet been laid.*

After His crucifixion, Jesus was laid in a tomb in a garden. There, His body, His flesh, was laid to rest.

> *Galatians 5:24*
> *And those who belong to Christ Jesus have crucified the flesh with its passions and desires.*

This garden tomb is the final resting place of our fleshly desires. As we grow in our walk with Jesus, we learn to take these passions and desires to this garden tomb and live in resurrection life.

> *Romans 6:5-7*
> *For if we have been united with Him in a death like His, we shall certainly be united with Him in a resurrection like His. We know that our old self was crucified with Him in order that the body of sin might be brought to nothing, so that we would no longer be enslaved to sin. For one who has died has been set free from sin.*

People want to live resurrection lives but aren't willing to die first. Many struggle with the garden tomb because they aren't willing to put their flesh into it. So rather than live in the new nature given to them, they chose to live dragging the dead body of their former passions and desires around with them and allowing the stench of the old nature to be the fragrance of their identity.

THE FOUNDATIONAL MOMENT IN OUR MOMENTUM

This first interaction with the clutch sets the tone for the *rest encounters* that we discussed earlier in the book. The clutch of this first gear creates the foundation for shifting through the rest of the Gears of Grace.

The discipline of laying to rest our fleshly desires forces a moment of pause, where we view our lives, issues, or temptations from a place where we have muzzled our fleshly cravings, removing their influence and silencing their voice to hear from the Spirit. In a sense, we remove the lens of the flesh and choose the lens of "Jesus is Lord".

This Garden tomb becomes a waypoint for our future clutch moments as it develops the practice and capacity to force our flesh to be quiet, and to hear from our Father for our journey as disciples.

YOU CARRY A FRAGRANCE

John 12:3

*Mary therefore took a **pound of expensive ointment** made from pure nard, and anointed the feet of Jesus and wiped his feet with her hair. **The house was filled with the fragrance of the perfume.***

When Mary performed this beautiful act of worship, the fragrance of the perfume filled the room. Have you ever been in a room where someone wore too much perfume? You can smell it everywhere, and inevitably it gets on you, and you end up smelling like the person wearing the perfume.

My friend Marlin Giesbrecht, years ago, shared how in a small village, word of this extravagant act of worship would have spread quickly through the town. He asked us then to imagine if we had been in the room and had seen what had happened and then left the room and were walking down the street soon after. And someone downwind from you gets a whiff of the perfume they had heard was just poured out on Jesus.

Marlin then told us to think of that person's response to the scent of the perfume. They would have thought, "That must be Jesus because I can smell the perfume." Only to turn around and see you.

Paul shared this same analogy to the Corinthians.

2 Corinthians 2:14-17 (ESV)
But thanks be to God, who in Christ always leads us in triumphal procession, and through us spreads the fragrance of the knowledge of him everywhere. For we are the aroma of Christ to God among those who are being saved and among those who are perishing, to one a fragrance from death to death, to the other a fragrance from life to life. Who is sufficient for these things? For we are not, like so many, peddlers of God's word, but as men of sincerity, as commissioned by God, in the sight of God we speak in Christ.

There is a fragrance coming off those living in resurrection life, and there is a fragrance coming off those carrying around death. So, which fragrance will you choose?

The definition of submission is the action or fact of accepting or yielding to a superior source or to the will or authority of another. It's the conscious decision that yielding to the superior is more favourable than asserting independence.

This clutch of submission removes the tension of living in a "sin cycle" not by overcoming a particular sin but by initiating the mindset of belonging entirely to Jesus. The first clutch of submission means to lay me to rest. It's not passive good intention but the conscious exercise of our will to die to our old selves.

MUSCLE MEMORY

Unlike a light switch, which can be turned off and on in an instant, renewing our minds is a process. Prior to becoming a follower of Jesus, our sinful nature trained us to react in sinful ways. It takes time to unlearn old habits and learn new ones. That muscle memory will "kick in" automatically at first and will feel more natural than a holy response. There will be times where we will repent for the same old habits, but we will grow and begin to ask for power to overcome (which we will look into a bit more in the next gear).

It may require prayer, accountability, inner healing, or even deliverance. The good news is that we're not alone. The Holy Spirit is with us and will guide us on our journey, showing us the way. Whether it's consistently turning away from something and turning to God, or a simple repentant act with power provided to overcome. Either way, we are invited to greater intimacy with the Holy Spirit and swift obedience to what He points out. In this way, sin cannot be a barrier to intimacy with God and you will not stay in the "sin cycle" of first gear.

1 Corinthians 6:19-20
*Or do you not know that **your body** is **a temple of the Holy Spirit** within you, whom you have from God?*

You are not your own, for you were bought with a price. So, glorify God in your body.

> Lack of submission is ultimately the assertion of our autonomy over Jesus' leadership in our lives.

The first and most crucial hurdle the disciple needs to navigate is independence. Lack of submission is ultimately the assertion of our autonomy over Jesus' leadership in our lives. This independence is what Paul challenges the Corinthians in 1 Corinthians 6:19-20. Until we come to grips with the fact that we are not our own, we will continue to claim ownership of ourselves, which robs us of lives of destiny.

CULTURE OF YES

Why is submission so important? Because the only appropriate response to Royalty is "Yes."

Jesus is the King of all kings. He is Royalty. And the adventure awaiting you at the speed of destiny depends upon your determined and unwavering "Yes" to the King.

Friend, the choice of Jesus is not just an invitation into eternal life but an invitation to die to all independence and become entirely submitted to Jesus. Don't be deceived into thinking discipleship's call to laying everything down is optional. It's like when a kid holds on to a cookie but can't get his hand out of the jar, not realizing he can have all the cookies if he lets go. We cannot receive all that God has for us while hanging on to what we want to keep of us. Any message that claims to be the gospel that doesn't invite you to lay everything down is a false gospel.

COMPARTMENTALIZATION'S ANTIDOTE

Compartmentalization is when we accept the Lordship of Jesus over some parts of our lives, but not others. Submission is the antidote to compartmentalization because it brings the whole of our hearts to honour the Lordship of Jesus. To move forward in the Gears of Grace, we must address where Jesus isn't Lord.

Perhaps you desire to know God more intimately and where He wants to lead you into destiny but have not been willing to address the tension you have felt in holding on to sin-patterned living. Today, you can engage the clutch of submission. Submit your life to Jesus and put the old self into the garden tomb where it belongs, and then you will begin to experience what overcoming and freedom feel like. Because the promise of God to the submitted heart is that submission causes the enemy to flee.

CLUTCH PRAYER – REPENT

Lord Jesus, I see the direction not submitting my life is leading me. I confess I have not been willing to surrender my life entirely to You. I repent. I ask Your forgiveness for trying to be Lord over my life in some areas and not letting You be Lord over all of my heart.

I choose submission. Your ways will always be better for me than my own, and I choose to hear and follow You. I now command my old nature to go into the tomb prepared for it, and I embrace Jesus as my Lord.

In Jesus' Name.

Amen

A QUICK REVIEW

The first Gear of Grace is God's Delight in Extending Mercy—the guarantee of forgiveness.

The tension is sin — Choosing to live in knowingly sinful patterns.

The Clutch-Submission-Deliberate submission to the Lordship of Jesus over our lives and finding our desires satisfied in Him rather than in sin.

Now, with submission engaged, let's move on to the next Gear of Grace, Managing Liberty.

STUDY QUESTIONS

How does living in deliberate sin affect your intimacy with God?

Why is submitting to the Lordship of Jesus over some areas so difficult?

In his great book, "Questions for Jesus," Tony Stoltzfus identifies four categories of desires and further breaks them down with four more expressions of those desires. They are listed below and they are common triggers for sin, as our old selves seek to satisfy them without God. Read through them and ask the Holy Spirit to reveal if any of these desires are presently being satisfied in your life through sin. Again, these desires are not sinful, but they can be met through sin, or anything that is not God's best for you:

1. Achievement
    - Justice
    - Freedom
    - Challenge
    - Significance
2. Connection
    - Worth
    - Be Known
    - Joy
    - Love

3. Stability
   - Belonging
   - Comfort
   - Peace
   - Security
4. Competence
   - Come Through
   - Goodness
   - Recognition
   - Approval[13]

Renew - What is the Holy Spirit saying about how Jesus can fulfill those desires? (Remember, the renewal of our minds is learning how Heaven thinks on a subject and then choosing that to be the truth we live out.)

Respond - What changes do you need to make in submission to shift out of first gear? (Reread the Garden Tomb.)

CHAPTER 4

SECOND GEAR: MANAGING LIBERTY

LIVING AS ONE WHO IS FREEBORN

1 Corinthians 6:12
"All things are lawful for me," but not all things are helpful. "All things are lawful for me," but I will not be dominated by anything.

THE SECOND GEAR OF GRACE IS MANAGING LIBERTY.

As we saw in first gear, there is more to the grace of God than the guarantee of forgiveness. So, when we learn to submit our lives to the Lordship of Jesus, we unlock the potential of the second Gear of Grace: the management of our liberty.

First, Paul wrote that all things are lawful, but not all things are helpful. The guarantee of forgiveness makes all things available to us. Why? Because we can simply lean into the grace of God and receive forgiveness. But they are not all helpful, which also means *to bring together*. All things may be lawful for us, but not all things bring us together with Jesus.

Second, Paul wrote that everything is lawful but wouldn't let anything dominate him. To be dominated means to be mastered or ruled over by something.

The incomplete message of grace that doesn't move beyond the first gear, leaves us enslaved to sin. We are empowered for victory over sin. And it is an insult to the character of God for His children to be in slavery.

It is an insult to the character of God for His children to be in slavery.

James 2:12

So speak and so act as those who are to be judged under the law of liberty.

CONFUSING

The term "law of liberty" is confusing. Having law and liberty in the same phrase seems contradictory, especially when "law" is immediately associated with religion.

We don't understand the power of the phrase "law of liberty" because we don't fully understand the meaning of the words shared. Jesus gave us a greater sense of what it means when He spoke of freedom from the gospel of John.

John 8:34-36

Jesus answered them, "Truly, truly, I say to you, everyone who practices sin is a slave to sin. The slave does not remain in the house forever; the son remains forever. So if the Son sets you free, you will be free indeed."

The words that Jesus used for *free* and *free indeed* are related, but they do not mean the same thing. When Jesus said, "if the Son sets you free," He used the verb *eleutheroo*, which means to liberate or make free. When He said, "free indeed," he used the adjective *eleutheros*, which means freeborn.

In other words, you are freeborn when the Son frees you from sin. This is why we are born again! We were each born into the slavery of sin. Jesus' death and resurrection freed us from that slavery, allowing a miraculous rebirth as freeborn men and women. Therefore, to be freeborn means not being born into slavery.

James uses another form of this word when he writes of the law of liberty. He uses the noun *eleutheria*, which means the liberty to do as one pleases but also to live as one should, not just as one pleases. It's also a word historically connected with the freeing of enslaved people. For example, upon the release of a Greek slave from slavery, the legal document contained the phrase "for freedom."

This is why this phrase, "law of liberty," is critical to understanding second gear. Paul wrote about this in Romans.

Romans 6:15-23

*What then? **Are we to sin because we are not under the law but under grace? By no means!** Do you not know that **if you present yourselves to anyone as obedient slaves, you are slaves of the one whom you obey**, either of sin, which leads to death, or of obedience, which leads to righteousness? But thanks be to God, that **you who were once slaves of sin have become obedient from the heart to the standard of teaching to which you were committed**, and, having been set free from sin, have become slaves of righteousness. I am speaking in human terms, because of your natural limitations. For just as you once presented your members as slaves to impurity and to lawless-*

ness leading to more lawlessness, so now present your
members as slaves to righteousness leading to sanctifi-
cation.

For when you were slaves of sin, you were free in
regard to righteousness. *But what fruit were you*
getting at that time from the things of which you are
now ashamed? For the end of those things is death. **But**
now that you have been set free from sin and have
become slaves of God, *the fruit you get leads to sancti-*
fication and its end, eternal life. **For the wages of sin is**
death, *but the free gift of God is eternal life in Christ*
Jesus our Lord.

JUDGED BY FREEDOM

The challenge to us from both James and Paul is to judge our lives
by this law of freedom.

Are we living like we are enslaved or like we are freeborn?

Freedom in Christ isn't expressed by simply leaning into God's
unending grace. Continually leaning into His grace while consciously choosing sin is a sign of slavery, not freedom. As I shared earlier,
our freedom is so complete that we can only be in bondage where we
choose to be in bondage. Paul confirms this when he points out that
presenting ourselves as obedient slaves leads to slavery. He does not
talk of being conquered by sin or losing battles to sin but instead giving
ourselves up as slaves to it.

Managing our liberty is frankly a "sin or not to sin" mindset. Now
there are two important things that I want to share with you. First,
this gear holds great value because it is in this gear we learn how to
walk as victors. However, this is not a gear of destiny speed. To reduce
your Christianity to simply a "sin or not to sin" lifestyle is like having

a bank account of a billion dollars and reducing it to what you could fit in your wallet. There is so much more to Christianity than living wondering if you should or shouldn't sin. Religion would like to keep your walk with Jesus stunted to this second-gear thinking, reducing your relationship with God to the old dance routine of "doing what's right to be accepted," which leaves us empty and powerless. While at the same time, permissiveness calls back from first gear, saying, "you're free to do whatever you want, don't be so religious."

Both are lies from the enemy robbing people of significance, peace, rest, love, and intimacy.

Paul challenges us to consider our actions' value and not allow ourselves to return to slavery.

I will repeat it; it is an insult to the character of God for His children to be enslaved to anything.

Slavery to sin is incompatible with the Cross.

FREEDOM IS RELATIVE

In today's thinking, truth is relative, meaning something might be true for you but not for me. It's a lie that is holding the lost captive to deception and being massaged into the thought patterns of modern-day Christians.

The relativity of truth is so destructive because relativity rejects Jesus as the Truth, and as a result, the Bible becomes relative. This is understandable for the lost, but it, unfortunately, has crept into the belief system of the Body of Christ, especially in the area of the grace of God.

For many in the body who have not progressed beyond first or second gear, truth is an opinion, whether or not the Word of God confirms it. In so doing, we have enthroned our intellect above the wisdom of God.

I heard Francis Chan say that whenever he finds himself disagreeing with something in the Bible, he immediately assumes something is wrong with him. What an incredible thought, and yet what an appropriate posture for a disciple. Jesus is the Word, and He is the final word on truth.

> *John 1:1-5*
>
> *In the **beginning was the Word**, and the **Word was with God**, and the **Word was God**. He was in the **beginning with God**. All things were made through Him, and without Him was not anything made that was made. **In Him was life, and the life was the light of men**. The light shines in the darkness, and the darkness has not overcome it.*

We will often find that the Word of God will offend our intellect and the pop culture of the day. It will offend anything not submitted to the Lordship of Jesus. I realize this is a hard truth to manage, but necessary to move beyond first and second gear.

Yet grace and truth find their perfection in the person of Jesus.

> *John 1:14*
>
> *And the **Word became flesh** and dwelt among us, and we have seen His glory, glory as of **the only Son from the Father, full of grace and truth**.*

So how do we manage this dichotomy between grace and truth, and how it relates to freedom? First, we return to the proper definition of the freedom given to us by Jesus. We are freeborn. Obeying the law of liberty, not being enslaved to anything.

Second, we invite the Holy Spirit to take the truth of Christ and make it known to us.

John 16:13-14

When the Spirit of truth comes, He will guide you into all the truth, for He will not speak on His authority, but whatever He hears He will speak, and He will declare to you the things that are to come. He will glorify Me, for He will take what is Mine and declare it to you.

Third, we no longer let truth be a moving target and let intimacy guide us.

Intimacy with Jesus is the best gauge of freedom. When truth is relative, it becomes a moving target. My truth, your truth, who's right? We know the answer is Jesus, but how do we measure it?

Intimacy.

Freedom is the moving target, not truth, and intimacy lets us know if we are on target. Think of it this way. Today consuming alcohol has become a topic of freedom. Some feel that complete abstinence is the godly response, others think that the occasional drink with a meal is healthy, while others feel that partying is okay.

Each camp proclaims its point of view as truth and defines behaviour as freedom. However, think of it this way. To one who has come out of a very legalistic atmosphere, a glass of wine with a meal might feel like freedom. Whereas to the alcoholic, no longer having to drink is freedom. Freedom then becomes relative. So how do we navigate through these waters?

First, we submit to the Word of God. If it is prohibited in the Word, then it is prohibited to disciples of the Word. Here is where the Holy Spirit will bring the Word of God alive to show how to live. Now there will be those who will look at some Old Testament laws to try to dispute what I have just written. However, Jesus fulfilled those laws of acceptance through performance. Jesus even spoke to the Pharisees about old covenant laws in the Gospel of John.

> *John 5:38-40*
> *"And you do not have His word abiding in you, for you do not believe the one whom He has sent. You search the Scriptures because you think that in them you have eternal life; and it is they that bear witness about Me, yet you refuse to come to Me that you may have life."*

The New Testament or New Covenant teachings of Jesus and the apostles give us clear direction regarding what new covenant living should look like.

Second, we measure how behaviour affects our intimacy with Jesus. If an activity corrupts an individual's intimacy with Jesus, then for that person, that behaviour isn't freedom.

Along with this law of liberty, as I have looked through the New Testament, I have found three other laws that help us navigate through the waters of grace and freedom, leading to intimacy, and have shared them in the Appendix.

THE TENSION: TEMPTATION, TO SIN OR NOT TO SIN, THAT IS THE QUESTION

Christians must overcome this tension to move beyond a boring lifestyle of saying no, to the incredible adventure of saying yes to what Kingdom living brings us as God's children.

The sin or not to sin lifestyle depends on two lies the enemy has peddled for ages.

God is Withholding from You

This first lie was what the enemy used as the first form of deception on humanity.

> *Genesis 3:1-5*
>
> *Now the serpent was more crafty than any other beast of the field that the Lord God had made.*
>
> *He said to the woman, "**Did God actually say, 'You shall not eat of any tree in the garden'?**" And the woman said to the serpent, "We may eat of the fruit of the trees in the garden, but God said, You shall not eat of the fruit of the tree that is in the midst of the garden, neither shall you touch it, lest you die.'" But the serpent said to the woman, "**You will not surely die. For God knows that when you eat of it your eyes will be opened, and you will be like God.**"*

Questioning the character of God is at the root of every lie the enemy sows our way. This is a vital part of the enemy's scheme to deceive any person. *God is withholding something from you.* When the enemy challenged Eve, it was to make her think God was holding something back from her.

To paraphrase the deception, "God doesn't want to share everything with you."

Temptation comes to us to convince us to meet our desires through sin. So, in a sense, the enemy challenges us, saying that God's way is withholding something from us and our desire will only be fully satisfied through sin.

James said it best when he described temptation and sin.

James 1:14-17

*But each person is tempted when he is **lured and enticed by his own desire**. Then desire when it has conceived gives birth to sin, and sin when it is fully grown brings forth death.*

Do not be deceived, my beloved brothers. Every good gift and every perfect gift is from above, coming down from the Father of lights with whom there is no variation or shadow due to change.

Every good gift comes from God. There's no changing in His character. This lie, that God is withholding from you, is diffused by faith. It is broken through resting in the belief that God is good, and He is not trying to rob us of anything.

Caught Between Two Conditions

The second lie this tension relies upon is the belief that our sinful nature causes us to be generally evil.

I used to joke with my congregation by saying I didn't have to practice sinning. I was seemingly a natural at it. So, we would laugh a little, and I would move on.

Then the Lord convicted me about conveying such terrible theology.

The fact of the matter is that our old sinful nature that we inherited from Adam is dead.

Romans 6:6-11

*We know **that our old self was crucified with Him** so that **the body of sin might be brought to nothing** so that **we would no longer be enslaved to sin**. For one who **has died has been set free from sin**. Now if we* *have died with Christ, we believe that we will also live with Him. We know that Christ, being raised from the dead, will never die again; death no longer has dominion over Him. For the death He died he died to sin, once for all, but the life He lives he lives to God. So* **you also must consider yourselves dead to sin and alive to God in Christ Jesus.**

You're a terrible sinner! You are just no good at it at all. Sin is the most unnatural thing for a follower of Jesus.

When we believe a part of us is still alive wanting sin, we live in one of two conditions. When we are holy and when we are evil. So, then we are certain sin is an inevitability and therefore, have to fight this inner battle having to choose to sin or not to sin.

When a person has had an amputation of a limb, they can experience what is called "phantom pain." Many amputees will go through a season where they can "feel" their amputated limb. Whether it is an itch or pain, they struggle with the real feeling of something that isn't there.

The enemy will come along disguised as your old nature, trying to convince you of the phantom itch of an old craving. But it isn't you!! That part of you doesn't exist anymore. You are freed from sin. The Cross and the covenant you're a part of as a disciple of Jesus frees you entirely of your old nature. You are freeborn!!

2 Corinthians 5:17
Therefore, if anyone is in Christ, he is a new creation. The old has passed away; behold, the new has come.

MIRROR THERAPY

> *When the image of Jesus defines us, it becomes gloriously simple to uncover the deception of the enemy.*

Often people will ask me how to discern when they are being tempted. The feelings they may have, like the phantom pain, would seem so real, and they are unsure if their old nature is truly dead. The answer is quite simple.

You and I are being conformed to Jesus' image according to Romans 8:29.

One of the forms of therapy for people suffering from phantom pain or itch is doing physical therapy in front of a mirror. That way, they can see the truth in front of them.

We need to do the same thing. Again, we are being conformed into an image. If you look into the image of Jesus and you don't see the activity you're being tempted by, then you know it's not in the new you.

When the image of Jesus defines us, it becomes gloriously simple to uncover the deception of the enemy.

ROY'S STORY

My friend Roy's story beautifully shows his journey in liberty.

I really can't remember a time not going to church. My first experience with God was that He was a harsh Judge and Ruler and always unhappy with me.

He was one to be feared.

In the same way, Jesus was always presented as the one we had to aspire to be like. Perfect and without any sin.

This led to me living under fear and condemnation. I felt like I could never live up to the perfect standard of Jesus, leading to the hopeless fear of God's eventual judgment.

My 'religion' was impossible, and I had no idea what God's true nature was like.

Then I experienced salvation through Jesus. This new encounter with the love of God, not His condemnation but His love, brought such freedom! Living in grace was so liberating at first because, suddenly, I knew that the love of God was what saved me, and God's grace was the expression of that love. This new understanding that Jesus died for me, sparing me from the lake of fire and judgment spoken of every Sunday in my upbringing, brought a new joy and peace. However, this is where a different journey began, which felt like a confusing maze. The journey into what is called liberty.

It started out slow, but the enemy's lies over the years led me to believe I could compare my walk with Jesus to others. In a sense letting relativism dictate my liberty. I began to think, "Well, they are living life this way and professing to be Christian, then it should be good for me to live that way too."

One specific example was the consumption of alcohol. I'm not making blanket statements about your journey or perspective, but where I grew up, it was generally forbidden. While my mom would always say it is not what goes into your mouth but what comes out of it that brings destruction, my experience was a bit different.

My limited understanding of the abundance of freedom and grace led me down a path where alcohol was controlling me rather than me controlling it.

I was reborn, but my identity was still a slave to sin. What's even more confusing is the further I desired to go away from religion through professing grace and freedom, the further I found myself away from intimacy with God.

It's a slippery slope, indeed. Over time, my businesses became everything to me, and the lure of wealth and luxurious living became what was most important to me. But, while these things are permissible under grace, they were slowly crowding out the still, small voice calling me back to intimacy. On the outside, everything appeared to be flourishing, but I wasn't.

Even so, I would continue to ignore that voice when I made decisions. Which eventually led to a string of decisions not very pleasing to God. And certainly not reflecting the faith that I professed. My mismanagement of the liberty I experienced through salvation was now keeping me in a sin or not to sin balancing act. If I chose to do a thing that was not life-producing, I would balance it out with an act of service that would create the illusion that I was still in God's good standing, like I was paying for my sin. I knew I was sinning, but I was deceived into thinking I could simply "pay God back" by doing good things to cover up my sin. In other words, religion. Pastor Landen always says that religion is performing in the hope of maintaining acceptance. And my form of repayment wasn't life-giving at all; it was tiring and boring.

Looking back, I can see how I was deceived. Thinking that getting what I wanted would give me what I needed.

But God wasn't done with me.

I knew there was more for me, and I began to long for the love that I knew in the early days of my journey with Jesus. The temptation was strong to try to meet that desire with the trappings that were available in business and wealth. But He began to reveal the Truth to me during my daily hike on a four-and-a-half-mile desert trail over a few months. I find it comical as I reflect on it. First, God literally took me to the desert to reach me in my spiritual desert. This is also where I was baptized in the Holy Spirit and received the gift of tongues. Then, after six months of crying out to God, He emptied me of all of me and refilled me with the Holy Spirit.

I realized that my faith was more than simply choosing to sin or not to sin. I began feeling a boldness and an unwillingness to compromise rising up in me. My repentance, or change of mind, became a resolve, resulting in a 180-degree shift in my direction. I began to allow the Holy Spirit to guide me and was willing to follow Him no matter the cost.

What a change this brought to my life and faith! I praise God daily for the fresh fire of the Spirit that He has put inside me. It has returned me to the first love I felt when I first found my freedom and redemption in Christ. Instead of resisting the still small voice, I recognize my helper, Holy Spirit, guiding and directing my path and constantly encouraging me to come closer to Him.

THE BIRTHPLACE OF RELIGION

Roy's story reveals how the spirit of religion works against the believer stuck in second gear. The proper stewardship of liberty brings a powerful sense of acceptance and love from God. However, when poorly stewarded, liberty can become the birthing place of the stronghold of religion in a believer's life.

When we are deceived into thinking sin can meet our needs the compromise of intimacy creeps into our lives; as a result, distance develops in our relationship with God. Broken intimacy allows performance to ease its wicked way into our lives. Performance leaves us feeling inadequate, hypocritical, and condemned to try to prove to God that we remain worthy of a relationship with Him.

So, we perform. We dance. We fight temptation outside of the strength of the Holy Spirit, living willfully and trying to meet our desires in our strength. Feeling the stress of our desires leading us further and further from God, we find ourselves relating to what Paul wrote in Romans 7.

Romans 7:21-24

*So I find it to be a law that when **I want to do right,** **evil lies close at hand.** For I delight in the law of God, in my inner being, **but I see in my members another law waging war against the law of my mind and making me captive to the law of sin that dwells in my members.** Wretched man that I am! Who will deliver me from this body of death?*

But Paul doesn't end there.

Romans 7:25 -8:2

***Thanks be to God through Jesus Christ our Lord!** So then, I myself serve the law of God with my mind, but with my flesh I serve the law of sin.*

There is therefore now no condemnation for those who are in Christ Jesus. For the law of the Spirit of life has set you free in Christ Jesus from the law of sin and death.

THE GARDEN OF EDEN – RETURNED TO OUR ORIGINAL DESIGN

When Adam and Eve were in the Garden of Eden, they were perfect. They had no flaw, created in the image of God. They didn't have a sinful nature, but *because they were deceived,* they sinned. And what was a perfect relationship with God was now corrupted by asserting their independence and sinning.

Through the Cross, we're invited to return to Eden. An invitation to return to the perfection that Adam and Eve were created in; the image and likeness of God (Genesis 1:26).

*To **put off your old self,** which belongs to your former manner of life and is **corrupt through deceitful desires,** and to be **renewed in the spirit of your minds** and to **put on the new self,** created after the likeness of God in true righteousness and holiness.*

What a powerful statement. *Created after the likeness of God in true righteousness and holiness.*

The Cross returns us to our original sinless design. That old nature is gone, and we can put on the new self, uncorrupted by sin, and through the strength of the Holy Spirit, empowered to live sin free, no longer subject to the slavery offered to us through temptation.

THE CURSE OF THE MIRROR

Earlier, I shared about conforming into the image of Jesus as a form to discern temptation, and it works. However, at the same time, there is an issue with the mirror that we have to address if we can truly experience the power of our original design and be an image bearer.

The problem with the mirror is we don't know how our image and the image of Jesus should be combined. On top of that, Satan deceives us into thinking that our reflection is our true condition.

And we generally don't like it.

We don't like it because we feel like those shortcomings that we see in the mirror make us unlovable. And if we don't fix those things, we don't qualify for love. So the enemy uses the mirror to establish a religious mindset, causing us to look in the mirror, speaking death over ourselves, cursing our image as unworthy, and never measuring up.

WORKING FROM LOVE RATHER THAN FOR LOVE

This became real for me one day as I passed by the mirror, looked at my reflection, and instantly criticized my appearance. The Lord stopped me in my tracks and said, "Landen, if you were to hear the compiled total of curses you have spoken over yourself, it would break your heart." I didn't quite understand what He meant, but He pressed me even further. He said, "It's breaking my heart, and I can't stand by any longer and allow you to be bullied like this anymore."

As is the case with God, He began to connect with me in my unconscious wounds, ministering to my heart, bypassing my consciousness. Suddenly the brokenness of my inner man, who had been subjected to this continual bullying, became very real to me, and I was overcome by emotion. As the tears welled up in my eyes, I felt the Lord say, "Do NOT declare what I have made holy to be unholy. Do NOT declare what I have made worthy of being unworthy. Do NOT declare what I have fashioned into my Son's image to be ugly when He is so beautiful, and Landen, do NOT reduce the work of the Cross in your life any longer. I love you, and you look like Me."

Working from love is way more effective than working for it. Therein is the difference between religion and grace.

We are meant to look fully like Jesus but fully like ourselves at the same time. As we are conformed into His image, we become our very best selves! Your best version of yourself looks fully like you, and Jesus can be fully seen in you.

I am not my dad. But as I age, I look more and more like he did, but I still look totally like me. And while I'm not Jesus, as I mature, I look more and more like Him and yet look fully like the very best version of me.

Perhaps, like me, you have spoken curses over the reflection in the mirror, robbing yourself of the wonder of seeing what God has designed your very best self to look like. So, take a moment and quiet your heart and ask Jesus this question.

Jesus, what is it about me that You love so much?

Get some tissues, turn on some worship, and enjoy the loving touch of God.

CLUTCH – STRENGTH: THE INTERNAL RESOLVE TO OVERCOME

> *Colossians 1:10-11*
> So as to **walk in a manner worthy of the Lord,** *fully pleasing to Him:* **bearing fruit in every good work** **and increasing in the knowledge of God;** *being* **strengthened with all power,** *according to His* **glorious might,** *for all endurance and patience with joy.*

> *Ephesians 3:16-17*
> *That* **according to the riches of His glory** *he may* **grant you to be strengthened** *with power through his Spirit* **in your inner being.**

As Roy did in his story, it's time for the Body of Christ to find its strength and resolve. The world is crying out for believers to be stronger than we are. Humility has been displayed as fearing greatness, and meekness has been defined as weakness.

The Holy Spirit isn't given to us to weaken us. There is no glory in weakness. Many of you might think of what Paul wrote to the Corinthians about boasting in weakness, for when "I am weak He is strong." Paul's purpose was to challenge us not to be strong in our own strength but to allow the strength of the Spirit to fill us. But somehow, we have thought we should be weak.

No way!

Lion Killers

1 Peter 5:8
*Be sober-minded; be watchful. **Your adversary, the Devil** prowls around **like a roaring lion, seeking someone to devour.***

We have heard this Scripture and been warned of our adversary's power. And indeed, he does prowl about intimidating God's people into believing they cannot defeat him, and he's looking to swallow up our resolve for victory.

However, let me declare this as clearly as possible.

You can be victorious over the Devil on any day that ends in a "y."

You don't need to be in church to have victory over him; you don't need to be "prayed up" to have victory over him; you don't need to be with friends to have victory over him. All of those things are good and important. But you are filled with the Holy Spirit who strengthens your inner being with all the strength of Heaven. You are not alone; you are in Christ and possess all the power you need to overcome. Consider the following verse Peter wrote.

1 Peter 5:9
***Resist him, firm in your faith,** knowing that the same kinds of suffering are being experienced by your brotherhood throughout the world.*

BE MIGHTY

The exploits of David's mighty men always leave me breathless. They were men who joined David while he hid in the caves of Adullam. Yet, when he took these men in, they were certainly not mighty.

> *1 Samuel 22:2*
>
> *And everyone who was **in distress**, and everyone who was **in debt**, and everyone who was **bitter in soul**, **gathered to him**. And he **became commander** over them. And there were with him about four hundred men.*

And yet, over time, that group of four hundred became a mighty army; out of them, thirty-three men rose to greatness and renown. They were so great they were called the mighty men. I want to look at one of them, whose name is Benaiah.

> *1 Chronicles 11:22-25*
>
> *And **Benaiah the son of Jehoiada** was **a valiant man** of Kabzeel, a **doer of great deeds**. He **struck down two heroes of Moab**. He also **went down and struck down a lion in a pit on a day when snow had fallen**. And he **struck down an Egyptian**, a **man of great stature, five cubits tall**. The Egyptian had in his hand a spear like a weaver's beam, but Benaiah went down to him with a staff and **snatched the spear out of the Egyptian's hand and killed him with his own spear**. These things did Benaiah the son of Jehoiada and **won a name beside the three mighty men**. He was renowned among the thirty, but he **did not attain to the three**. And David set him over his bodyguard.*

Whoa. Those are some great deeds, indeed! Benaiah was a serious dude, and yet, he didn't attain to the three. Do you want to be inspired? Read through David's mighty men.

If David could call out such greatness in men who were distressed, in debt, and depressed, how much more should Christ in us, the hope of glory, call greatness out of you and me?

Humility is not avoiding greatness; it is greatness that doesn't need glory. Meekness isn't weakness. It is great strength under control.

> *Ephesians 6:10-14a*
>
> *Finally, **be strong in the Lord and in the strength of His might**. Put on the whole armour of God, that **you may be able to stand against the schemes of the Devil**. For we do not wrestle against flesh and blood, but against the rulers, against the authorities, against the cosmic powers over this present darkness, against the spiritual forces of evil in the heavenly places. Therefore take up the whole armour of God, that **you may be able to withstand** in the evil day, and **having done all, to stand. Stand therefore...***

CLUTCH PRAYER – REPENT

Lord Jesus, I am done with being satisfied with weakness. I have believed the lie of being still subject to my old nature. I declare that my old sinful nature is dead, and I am a new creation in Jesus. I repent for believing that weakness was satisfactory, and I ask you to strengthen me in my inner man. I ask You to empower me through grace to overcome temptation and live freeborn.

I thank you for strengthening me. Let my life be a wonderful act of worship to you.

In Jesus' Name,

Amen

The clutch of strength will address the tension of temptation and allow you to shift into the next Gear of Grace. Authority.

A Quick Review

The second gear of grace is the management of our liberty.

The tension is temptation—to sin or not to sin. The key is if it doesn't look like Jesus, it doesn't look like me.

The clutch is strength—the internal resolve to overcome.

Study Questions

How does living in a 'sin or not to sin' mentality rob one of experiencing joy and peace in their journey with Jesus?

Why has the enemy's strategy of deceiving believers to choose to live in sin patterns remained so effective?

Look over the list of desires once again. Which desires is the enemy trying to tempt you to meet through sin?

1. Achievement
   - Justice
   - Freedom
   - Challenge
   - Significance
2. Connection
   - Worth
   - Be Known
   - Joy
   - Love
3. Stability
   - Belonging
   - Comfort
   - Peace
   - Security

4. Competence
   - Come Through
   - Goodness
   - Recognition
   - Approval[14]

Renew – In what areas is the Holy Spirit challenging you about where you live from weakness instead of strength? (Remember, the renewal of our mind is learning what Heaven is saying about a thing and making that the truth we live in.)

Respond – In what ways is the Holy Spirit challenging you to fulfill those desires by living from your original design? (Reread the Garden of Eden.)

CHAPTER 5

THIRD GEAR: AUTHORITY

FINDING YOUR PURPOSE

Colossians 2:9-10

*For **in Him** the whole fullness of deity dwells bodily, and **you have been filled in Him**, who is the Head of all rule and authority.*

Luke 7:6-10

*And Jesus went with them. When He was not far from the house, the centurion sent friends, saying to Him, "Lord, do not trouble Yourself, for I am not worthy to have you come under my roof. Therefore I did not presume to come to You. But say the word, and let my servant be healed. **For I too am a man set under authority, with soldiers under me: and I say to one, 'Go,' and he goes; and to another, 'Come,' and he comes; and to my servant, 'Do this,' and he does it."** When Jesus heard these things, He marvelled at him, and turning to the crowd that followed Him, said, "I tell you, not even in Israel have I found such faith."*

> *And when those who had been sent returned to the house, they found the servant well.*

> *Luke 10:19-20*
> *"Behold, I have given you authority to tread on serpents and scorpions, and over all the power of the enemy, and nothing shall hurt you. Nevertheless, do not rejoice in this, that the spirits are subject to you, but rejoice that your names are written in Heaven."*

THE THIRD GEAR OF GRACE IS AUTHORITY. IT'S THE STEWARDship of more than just a personal faith that can remain hidden from the world. It becomes a faith that merges onto the freeway of destiny.

In third gear, you are speeding up and covering significant ground in your maturity.

ACTIVATED – DO THEY KNOW YOU IN HELL?

I spent a summer at a Moose Lake Camp in Northern Alberta when I was thirteen. It was my first foray into leadership. I was a camp counsellor for a week at their children's camp.

During one of the evening services during the week, an incident happened that would profoundly affect my life.

I witnessed my first demonic manifestation.

A youngster at camp suddenly started screaming at leaders, swearing and calling us sinners. She was wild-eyed and growling and speaking in an eerie gravelly voice. The strength that the demon manifested through the young girl was astounding. It took six men to hold her down while she frothed at the mouth, growling, and snapping at us while shouting profanities and accusations.

We have learned much about how to manage these incidents since then, but back in that day, the ones who yelled loudest would be the eventual winners. So, we were yelling, she was yelling, and not much was happening.

Then there was a short lull in the action, and she got an evil gleam in her eyes and began to speak quietly in that raspy voice. Through her, the demon started to threaten different leaders, saying how it would terrorize this person and that person.

Then in that same ominous tone, it said, "And I am going to get... Landen."

I froze, the hair on the back of my neck stood up, and fear gripped me, making my insides tremble.

A more seasoned leader must have seen my ashen face, leaned over, and said, "It's only trying to intimidate you."

Well, it worked.

I was scared out of my mind.

We eventually cast that demon out, and the lovely youngster returned to the precious girl we knew before, except now she was totally free.

I, however, was a basket case. I mean, a demon, a demon from hell, said MY name. I had never prayed so much in my life. I didn't sleep much that night. Every snap and creak I heard was the hordes of hell coming to torture and haunt me for the rest of my days.

After one terrifying sound, I think it was a cow mooing in the distance (cut me some slack; I was pretty freaked out); the Lord spoke to me.

He said, "Landen, if they don't know you in hell, you mustn't be doing much for Heaven. Take it as a compliment. Hell is intimidated by you."

That one encounter brought two important revelations to me. First, it brought into light the full realization of how real the spirit realm is, and the second was that I was a player in God's plan, so much so that the enemy was intimidated by me.

The third gear of authority is the first fruit of an activated believer. It's the start of a disciple moving from a spectator to a participant in the grand plans of Heaven for God's Kingdom to be manifest on Earth.

An immediate mistake many make is to assume this authority will result in some form of leadership. Since we tend to think of promotion and position, we miss the true power of the authority given to us.

The Scriptures at the beginning of this Chapter show us we are filled with Him, who is authority. Our authority is never established through a position or promotion; it is always established in Jesus. Your inner conditions will not be affected by promotion. Many folks feel like victory over temptation lies just on the other side of a position in ministry, some form of ministry promotion, or any form of recognition from people.

Authority will always be a condition before it leads to a position.

Authority will always be a condition before it leads to a position. When the Centurion's friends spoke with Jesus in Luke 7, they shared the Centurion's understanding of who Jesus was. A man who was *under* authority. He understood Jesus was walking under the authority of God. You can declare promotion or even possess a position, but the authority of Heaven is possessed only by those who are under it.

This authority manifests itself first in the realm of the Spirit. When we, as disciples, move beyond a simple sin or not to sin mentality, we become threatening to the enemy. Not just because we are walking in our personal freedom, which is terrific, but because we are now carriers of freedom. Those disciples living freeborn will consistently see the promises of Jesus realized in their lives.

Mark 16:17-18
> *"And these **signs will accompany those who believe:** in My Name, they will cast out demons; they will speak in new tongues; they will pick up serpents with their hands; and if they drink any deadly poison, it will not hurt them; they will lay their hands on the sick, and they will recover."*

Many disciples don't use this Gear of Grace. They may use the clutch of strength to fight against temptation to sin but then coast for a moment and reengage the second gear of managing liberty without moving into authority. There are two reasons for this. The first is they think authority is positional, and because they aren't a pastor, minister, or ministry leader of something, they don't qualify to move into authority.

The belief that destiny is only found in vocational ministry is a wicked lie we must overcome if the world is going to experience the goodness of God. No line separates the "work of the Lord" from regular life. It is all meant to be the work of the Lord. You have a purpose right where you are right now. You can live in authority and operate in the anointing of Heaven in life right now.

This lie, which the Devil has so effectively sowed, robs people of impactful, inspiring lives by keeping them in a gear that can't manage the speed of destiny. Instead, they slow down and wave from the merging lane and watch others pass them into purpose, all the while feeling like the Lord is passing over them while others who are more gifted or influential go and change the world. They feel like their identity is lost, question their value, and quietly return to a life spent just overcoming sin.

When Paul wrote to the Ephesians, he clarified the purpose of ministry positions.

Ephesians 4:11-14
*And **He gave** the apostles, the prophets, the evangelists, the shepherds and teachers, **to equip the saints for the work of ministry,** for building up the Body of Christ, until we all **attain to the unity of the faith** and the **knowledge of the Son of God, to mature manhood,** to the measure of the stature of the fullness of Christ.*

Ministers, like coaches, are equippers to bring people to maturity to live like ministers worldwide. To view ministry as the privilege of only the pastoral team is to limit Jesus' work to the church's four walls. In essence, we are saying ministry only takes place on Sunday.

The second reason is rooted in fear. The fear is that if Christians move away from a religion of dos and don'ts, God will require everything of them, and they will be miserable serving Him. This fear is really a facade. What is happening is disobedience masquerades as fear which, in a sense, justifies our disobedience. Or, said another way, since I am afraid it is okay not to do what God asks.

After all, to follow God means to sell everything, give up your dreams, move to some mission field, and live in a hut. Which, of course, isn't true. God wants you fully engaged in life, absolutely filled with joy, purpose, and fulfilment in every way.

Jesus revealed the result of believing this lie in the parable of the talents.

Talents and Service

The authority that we are given can grow. Like any gift of the Kingdom of Heaven, we are responsible for stewarding what is given to us with integrity so that it grows.

Jesus explained it in the parable of the talents in Matthew 25. A master was leaving and gave three of his servants' talents to do business with until he returned. He gave to each of them according to their ability. To one, he gave five talents; to another, he gave two. And to another, he gave one. Upon his return, he found that those with five and two talents had doubled their money. He was pleased and said he could give them more. However, the one given the one talent hid it and returned it using his fear of the master as an excuse for his poor stewardship. The master was furious, saying if the servant were really afraid of his master, he would have at least invested it for some return. Then the master gave his servant's one talent to the one who already had ten.

Again, we are responsible as servants of God to use what He has given us so that our anointing and authority can grow. Whether you are a five-talent or one-talent person, the gifts of God are meant to grow. Like seeds have the potential of a harvest, so does the authority God gives you.

By the way, the growth of Kingdom gifts makes leadership at some level inevitable. Your good stewardship of what God gives you will open unexpected doors giving you influence and the opportunity to lead. It's called favour.

Why? Because Heaven's solutions to humanity's problems are one anointed person away from being realized. And you can be that person.

The Kingdom of God is a practical as well as a spiritual one. The principles of Heaven solve Earth's problems, and the King prefers to share His ways with the world through His kids!

How, then, do we handle this favour? Fortunately, God has provided a way for us to handle favour so that we can again show off His goodness.

> *Mark 10:42-44*
>
> *And Jesus called them to Him and said to them, "You know that **those who are considered rulers of** the Gentiles **lord it over them,** and their great ones exercise authority over them. **But it shall not be so among you.** But whoever would be great among you **must be your servant,** and whoever would be first among you must be slave of all.*

Jesus showed His disciples that in His Kingdom, leaders serve. Those in leadership must care for those who they have authority over. This principle of servant leadership is how we manage authority so we lead in a Kingdom fashion when given the opportunity.

THE TENSION – TEMPTATION: MY WAY OR GOD'S WAY

The third gear, Authority, finds its tension in temptation, but not to sin from the traditional sense of doing something wrong, but to sin by asserting independence.

As we steward our authority, having a clear sense of submission given to us in the first gear of grace becomes vital. Many have fallen victim to the temptation of sidestepping the ways of God to operate in independence, being deceived into thinking somehow their way of doing things would be better than Jesus'.

ARIELE'S STORY

One of the leaders of our dance ministry at Gateway is Ariele. Her story of learning to pursue God's way instead of her own is an excellent example of the tension that temptation can bring.

Growing up, I had three childhood dreams: to be a ballerina, a missionary, and finally, a mom. This third gear of authority is deeply intertwined with those dreams. I gave up ballet shortly after high school as I thought I could only pursue dance professionally. While I found ways to bless kids around me, becoming a mother depended not only on me but on the necessary other person who needed to be in the picture to make that happen. So then, naturally, all of my desires began to centre around going somewhere, anywhere, for any length of time, to take care of orphaned children and be a missionary.

I went on several short-term mission trips in high school, ultimately leading me to attend a Discipleship Training School through Youth With A Mission (YWAM). The school involved close relationships with fellow believers and travelling to Vancouver, Thailand, and Indonesia. We spent time ministering to little kids at children's homes at these places. I loved every minute of it, even the hard parts. But despite my and YWAM's best efforts to prepare me for my return home, I crashed emotionally. In the following nine months, I tried hard to find a place where I 'fit'—where my dreams for my life could be satisfied at my home in Edmonton.

At the end of the nine months, I decided in my heart that my dissatisfaction at home was a solid reason to leave again and go overseas or anywhere. So, I applied as a volunteer for another missions organization but was told I'd have to wait a year before they'd have any openings. Looking back, that setback was such a minor thing, but it felt soul crushing at the time. I felt like I had no purpose in life, and everything worked against me.

Then I heard God clearly tell me that He wanted me to stay home. That brought no comfort to me at all. Instead, I felt betrayed and became angry and bitter with God. Suddenly I had a place to dump all my hurt. To think that he would deny what I wanted most and, on top of that, make me stay in the "frozen wasteland" I resentfully called Edmonton.

How I wish I had responded to his promptings better! But I didn't. As a result, I made it incredibly painful for myself. I blamed God for everything I didn't understand and buried all my seemingly crushed dreams. I vowed to leave them behind and let them rot "since God didn't care about them."

Slowly I came to a place of hopeless resignation and took on the identity of an apathetic servant, mindlessly obeying what Heaven's taskmaster said to do. I would think, "Clearly, my job is just to do what God wants because what I want is out of the question." To soothe my soul, I began to pretend I had no desires. It was easier that way because I still wasn't understanding what God was doing.

I understand now that God saw the condition of my heart. He saw how I had become completely caught up in a desperate need to belong and to find identity in doing missions work. So, He firmly closed the door to what I thought I wanted and showed me another way—the way to His heart.

Here is something odd about that journey. Despite my anger, I was still having encounters with tangible love and the presence of God like never before. Even in my brokenness, He constantly revealed Himself, reminding me of His love even as I yelled at Him for breaking my heart. I weep now as I look back on all I accused Him of doing wrong. I saw what I know now was my loving, gentle, protective Abba Father as a vindictive overseer who gave hope only to take it away.

I am so thankful that God never quits on us, even when we feel like He has, or even when we give up. He continued loving, caring for, and speaking kindly to me. Slowly I found my way back to my abiding place in my loving Abba Father. The desire to belong and the identity I was searching for was found in Him, not in missionary work, or becoming a mother, or in dance. And as God became the solid foundation for my identity, He began to fulfill my dreams.

It's a pleasant surprise when you finally lay things down to find God standing before you, offering them back! And it is no longer broken and crushed but beautiful, whole, and vibrant!

At the end of the nine months, I joined the discipleship school of Gateway Family Church called School of Kingdom Life. After being there for about five months, the Lord returned my dream of being a dancer! But this time, it wasn't simply performing ballet but the chance to pioneer Gateway's dance ministry. I was shocked when Pastor Landen approached me and asked if I would lead it. In the past, I would have felt like I had to muscle my way into my desires, but after God refined my heart, He was just handing it to me as a gift from Him. In fact, the whole journey of leading this ministry, though I was fearful in the beginning, has been so incredibly effortless. And because of the refined nature of my heart to do these things His way instead of my way, I have grown much in the process, and so have the ministry and the people in Gateway Dance. Everything I've done seems prepared, simply waiting for me to pick it up at the right time.

I learned a hard lesson in submission. As I submit to His authority, He releases authority to my life. It was a hard lesson, but I am incredibly grateful for it. It has solidified my identity, grown my patience, and taken my intimacy with Jesus to incredible new depths. In hindsight, if I had gone overseas back then, I would have faced far more significant challenges. Instead of learning to find my identity at home in a culture I know, with friends around me, I would have lived the same journey in a strange place with unfamiliar people and risked coming home even more broken.

I'm still waiting on God for the day when he says, "Go," but I'm waiting in an entirely different posture. I'm at peace. And in the meantime, I get to lead these amazing dancers into what God has for us and Gateway. I also grew in another recently fulfilled dream: my relationship with my amazing husband and our two children. Now, I look forward with hope and excitement to what we will get to do together, and I am confident that at whatever time it happens, it will be absolutely amazing. I have no problem waiting anymore, nor any doubts that it will happen in His perfect time.

The great value of overcoming the temptation of doing things my way versus God's way is He protects our identity from being wrapped up in what we do instead of who we are. When we submit ourselves to His way of operating, He solidifies our identity in Him, which protects us from having to be doing something to be somebody.

I share this because so many disciples hope they gain an identity through their actions. Hoping their activity will give them an identity; however, they have it backward; their identity is supposed to result in activity.

Purpose doesn't create identity, but identity will create purpose.

THE GARDEN OF GETHSEMANE

The Garden of Gethsemane reveals the tension of this third gear.

Mark 14:35-36

*And going a little farther, He fell on the ground and prayed that, if it were possible, the hour might pass from Him. And He said, "Abba, Father, all things are possible for You. Remove this cup from Me. Yet **not what I will, but what You will.**"*

We access the authority of Heaven through submission. Authority isn't positional; it isn't relational, nor is it based on anointing. It is determined and established in a commitment to be wholly submitted to the Lordship of Jesus.

We can't be trusted with Heaven's authority without being submitted to Heaven's ways.

This tension that we feel is rooted in self-protection. It isn't so much an issue with independence leading to sin but rather an independence that guards us against the perceived difficulty of God's way.

> *We can't be trusted with Heaven's authority without being submitted to Heaven's ways.*

Matthew 16:25
For whoever would save his life will lose it, but whoever loses his life for My sake will find it.

Establishing a lifestyle of authority is one of the most challenging wrestling matches believers face because it is found by laying their lives down and trusting in Jesus' protection. This isn't just a "hedge of protection" type of prayer. It's the radical trust of literally laying our lives in His hands, determining not to lift a finger in self-protection.

In today's North American Christianity, there are three demonic strongholds firmly set in opposition to the Kingdom of Heaven being realized by the church. The first is self-preservation which is the root of compartmentalized hearts. These hearts embrace the Lordship of Jesus in some areas but not all. Thereby creating pockets in our hearts where we consciously do not submit to Jesus. The second, self-interest, is the root of consumerism, which reduces the Body of Christ to a provider of goods and services. It celebrates a connection that is contractual in nature. I will show up and tithe (or tip), and the church must entertain my needs, or I will find another place that meets them better. Instead of a covenant relationship of what we can bring to the Body of Christ, we have a contractual arrangement for what we can take. Finally, the third is self-protection, which is the root of individualism. Individualism manifests in two forms. The first is in the lie that we have individual relationships with Jesus. We do not. We are born into a family. We may have an intensely personal relationship with Jesus, but it's not an individual one. He will relate with us personally but not individually. He will always consider you personally but through the lens of the Body. That's why Paul wrote,

> *1 Corinthians 12:18-*
> *But as it is, **God arranged the members in the Body,** each one of them, **as He chose.** If all were a single member, where would the Body be? As it is, **there are many parts, yet one Body.***

The second form that individualism takes is acting independently of God's will. It's exalting what I think will be best above what God says will be best.

BACK TO THE GARDEN...

When Jesus was praying in the garden of Gethsemane, He battled the tension of this gear on our behalf. He had an opportunity to succumb to self-protection but chose to submit entirely to the will of God willingly. As a result, Jesus received complete authority.

> *Philippians 2:6-11*
> *Who, though **He was in the form of God,** did not count equality with God a thing to be grasped, but emptied Himself, by taking the form of a servant, being born in the likeness of men. And being found in human form, **He humbled himself by becoming obedient to the point of death, even death on a cross.** Therefore **God has highly exalted Him** and bestowed on Him the **Name that is above every name,** so that at the **Name of Jesus every knee should bow,** in Heaven and on Earth and under the earth, and every*

> **tongue confess that Jesus Christ is Lord,** to the glory
> of God the Father.

So how do we do this?

It's A Faith Thing

2 Corinthians 5:7
*For we walk **by faith, not by sight.***

The third gear of authority will constantly challenge us to walk by faith and not by what we see. Jesus saw the Cross coming in the garden, but, He chose to see what the Lord was doing *through* the cross.

There are times in the gear of authority when we will face the temptation to do things our way versus the way God has determined. What we do with that tension will determine whether or not we will see the talents grow.

This faith walk refines our faith for later gears.

Let's simplify faith to make it a part of our experience and more relaxed and consistent.

Hebrews 11:6
*And **without faith, it is impossible to please Him,** for*
*whoever would draw near to God **must believe** that*
He exists and that He rewards those who seek Him.

We use faith and belief interchangeably. But in Hebrews 11, we see two different words. Faith, or *pistis*, can also be described as being convinced. Whereas belief, *pisteuo*, infers commitment.

Consider this as an example. When we see a chair, we have faith or are convinced it will hold us. We exercise our belief in that faith when we commit to sitting in the chair. Faith is *being convinced*; belief is committing because we *are convinced*. This is why faith without works is dead. Being convinced means nothing if we are not prepared to commit through our actions.

We show we are walking in our faith when we act in belief. When we assert our independence by choosing our way instead of God's, we step out of belief because we are unwilling to commit to following His ways. The reason? We don't possess the faith, or in other words, we aren't convinced.

This makes Jesus' comments about faith like a mustard seed frustrating. In my book, *Renovated for Glory*, I discuss this subject at length, but for our conversation, I will share a couple of critical thoughts to help us on our journey.

First, faith is not the currency of Heaven. That bad theology results in thinking we must muster enough faith to get the Father's attention for Him to respond to us. In essence, when we have enough faith, we can purchase our breakthrough. This religious perspective of faith only affirms a works-based mentality. That is not the faith of a mustard seed Jesus was referring to.

The great faith that Jesus wants us to possess is found in His resurrection.

> *Romans 4:23-24*
> But the words "it was counted to him" were not written for his sake alone, but for ours also. **It will be counted to us who believe in Him who raised from the dead Jesus our Lord.**

If you are convinced in the gospel, the good news of the resurrection, you possess the faith needed to move mountains. Rather than basing our faith on the feeling of belief, we base it on the fact of Jesus' resurrection.

Whenever you find a challenge in front of you that makes you waver between choosing self-protection over the will of God, be encouraged! If you are convinced in the resurrection, you possess the faith you need to commit to the will of God. Bill Johnson wrote that "well stewarded faith increases faith itself."[15] David's victory over Goliath is a great example of growing faith. Scripture tells us that David had faith to go after Goliath on behalf of Israel because he had already killed both the lion and the bear (1 Sam. 17:35-36). He tells Saul in verse 37 that he knew it was God who had given him those victories, so he was prepared to face Goliath. Exercising our faith activates partnership with God and as a result our faith in Him grows. This isn't meant to become presumptive, and we'll talk about that later, but it's meant to be assertive, faith-filled obedience.

> *Galatians 2:20*
> *I have been crucified with Christ. It is no longer I who live, but Christ who lives in me. **And the life I now live in the flesh I live by faith in the Son of God,** who loved me and gave Himself for me.*

THE CLUTCH – PURPOSE

> *John 18:11*
> *So Jesus said to Peter, "Put your sword into its sheath; **shall I not drink the cup that the Father has given Me?"***

I love how the Message version shows Jesus' commitment to the will of the Lord.

John 18:11 (MSG)

Jesus ordered Peter, "Put back your sword. **Do you** **think for a minute I'm not going to drink this cup** **the Father gave me?"**

Immediately after Jesus makes His commitment to follow the will of His Father, He faces one more opportunity to abort the Cross by having His disciples violently protect Him. But His decision to follow His Father's plan had already started, and He engaged the clutch, His purpose. The tension was gone, and the resolve to see the will of God completed was His possession.

And Jesus commanded the swords of self-protection to be put away.

Jesus' commitment to live out His purpose dissolved the tension of deviating from the plan of God.

PURPOSE AND IDENTITY

John 12:27-32 (ESV)

"Now is My soul troubled. And what shall I say? *'Father, save Me from this hour'? **But for this purpose** **I have come to this hour.** Father, glorify Your Name."* *Then a voice came from Heaven: "I have glorified it,* *and I will glorify it again." The crowd that stood there* *and heard it said that it had thundered. Others said,* *"An angel has spoken to Him." Jesus answered, **"This** **voice has come for your sake, not Mine.** Now is the* *judgment of this world; now will the ruler of this world* *be cast out. And I, when I am lifted up from the Earth,* *will draw all people to Myself."*

Jesus was completely secure in His identity as God's Son. I share this because finding identity in purpose is unhealthy, but true health is when identity reveals purpose. Being clear in our hearts about who we are, sets us free from performance as our value which robs us of our true identity as children of God.

Scripture shows us that Jesus was consciously aware of His identity. While He humbled Himself to take on human form, temporarily laying down the prerogatives of His divinity (such as omnipresence and taking on human needs such as sleep and the bathroom), He was still consciously aware of His pre-birth existence. The first example is when He was twelve, and His parents found Him in the temple.

Luke 2:49

*And He said to them, "Why were you looking for me? Did you not know that **I must be in my Father's house?"***

John 17 reveals another hint toward Jesus' conscious awareness of His heavenly past.

John 17:5

*And now, Father, glorify Me in Your own presence **with the glory that I had with you before the world existed.***

This is the genius of the gospel. Jesus, fully God, laid down the privilege of the power He possessed as a member of the Trinity so that He could be filled with the Holy Spirit (See Luke 4:14), modelling for humanity how we can live filled with the Spirit. Still, all the time retaining His conscious knowledge of His eternal glory.

Again, can you see the brilliance of the completeness of God's gospel? Jesus already possessed a renewed mind. He faced all temptation from the position of knowing the truth of Heaven. Think of it. It even makes Satan's awkward attempts at temptation seem so futile. How do you convince this Jesus, who is entirely flesh but possessing a renewed mind, to sin?

Here God reveals a massive truth through the tactic used by Satan to tempt Jesus. Two of the three attempts to tempt Jesus to sin started by challenging who He was. Years ago, Amy Ball, our children's pastor at the time, asked one of our Gateway kids why we sin. This little girl, who has grown into a powerful prophetic young woman, answered, "Sometimes we forget who we are." What a revelation! Satan started his temptation with "If you are the Son of God," in Luke 4:3 and 9. How do you get a person with a renewed mind to sin? Get them to forget who they are and question their true identity.

> *1 Corinthians 2:15-16*
> **The spiritual person judges all things but is himself to be judged by no one. "For who has understood the mind of the Lord so as to instruct Him?" But we have the mind of Christ.**

In the late 300s, the early church fathers rejected a heresy called Apollinarianism. The heresy denied that Jesus had a natural mind but instead had "the Logos taking its place."[16] I'm not suggesting that Jesus didn't have a natural mind; I'm suggesting that His knowledge of who He was as the Son of God took precedence over His natural mind, in the same way that our knowledge of who we are as God's children and Heaven's ways and truths are meant to take precedence over our natural minds.

Here is where it gets exhilarating for us. We are liberated from sin to live the same way as Jesus. The Cross and water baptism completely free us from sin, allowing us to be born again or freeborn. But we also have access to the same mind as Christ, the renewed mind. So just like Jesus lived in the flesh, filled with the Spirit, consciously aware of His Heavenly existence, we can live in the same condition.

Ephesians 2:5-8

Even when we were dead in our trespasses, [He] made us alive together with Christ—by grace you have been saved—and raised us up with Him and seated us with Him in the heavenly places in Christ Jesus, so that in the coming ages He might show the immeasurable riches of His grace in kindness toward us in Christ Jesus.

I will take a moment to boast about my hero Jesus the Christ.

Often, we reduce our revelation to the life of Jesus to the three years of His life recorded in the Gospels. And while I am not suggesting that we ask for extra-biblical revelation on His unrecorded life, I am asking that we consider that there is a thirty-year window in the life of Jesus that we know nothing about, except we know what He did.

I recently listened to a message John Wimber shared before he passed away. He shared Mark's record of Jesus' baptism.

Mark 1:9-11

In those days Jesus came from Nazareth of Galilee and was baptized by John in the Jordan. And when He came up out of the water, immediately He saw the heavens being torn open and the Spirit descending on Him like a dove. And a voice came from Heaven, "You are My beloved Son; with You I am well pleased."

Wimber said something that I think we know and yet perhaps forget when we consider the life of Jesus.

The Heavens opened, and God spoke audibly about Jesus, declaring He was His beloved Son and that as His Father, He was pleased with Jesus. You may have heard it shared that Jesus had done nothing of Messianic value at that point because He hadn't started His public ministry. And God affirmed who Jesus was, and that He was loved even though He had done nothing in ministry yet.

And this is true. This powerful picture is a testimony of how much God loves us. Our value isn't based on what we have done but on who we are to Him. But Wimber revealed something I had never really considered, which opened my eyes to the magnificence of Jesus.

He said that while Jesus had done nothing of any Messianic ministry value, He fulfilled His Messianic calling by presenting Himself pure.

And while we don't know what He did, on account of His purity, we know that He lived sin free.

Hebrews 4:15
For we do not have a High Priest who is unable to sympathize with our weaknesses, but One who in every respect has been tempted as we are, yet without sin.

Our hero, Jesus, lived for thirty years facing every temptation we face, overcoming them all. He lived a life we could have never lived because He knew who He was. Since He knew who He was, He was uniquely equipped to overcome sin on our behalf throughout His childhood and teen years and as a carpenter during His work-a-day life.

This element of the gospel gets overlooked, and I think it holds a beautiful truth about the overcoming power of obtaining the mind of Christ. Jesus' full conscious knowledge of Heaven's ways and nature helped Him decide how He would respond to every temptation.

Therefore Jesus, fully aware of His Heavenly identity, lived what we could never live, to obtain for us what we could never acquire through our own fleshly attempts.

And because He knew who He was, He could lay down any independent willfulness that would move Him off the mark of God's plan since He was fully engaged in His purpose.

What is your purpose?

Purpose, to the religious, is simply found in doing what's right versus what's wrong. Purpose for those who are determined to walk in the authority of Heaven is revealed when Jesus taught us to pray, "Your Kingdom come, Your will be done on Earth as it is in Heaven."

Matthew 13:33
*He told them another parable. "The **Kingdom of Heaven is like leaven** that a woman took and hid in three measures of flour, **till it was all leavened.**"*

Jesus' point is that the Kingdom of Heaven, like the yeast affecting the whole lump of dough, can be expressed in every area of life. This truth blurs the line between the secular and sacred, making our entire lives sacred. God wants His Kingdom manifest at your job, in your school, at the hockey rink, and anywhere you are. He wants to be present so that people around you can see Christ in you, the hope of glory.

Bringing the Kingdom to every element of our lives becomes the purpose of those who engage the gear of authority. We find purpose when we live on purpose.

CLUTCH PRAYER

Lord Jesus, thank You for revealing the areas in my life where I am walking independently. Thank You for showing me where I am protecting myself, not by faith, and committing to what I know to be true.

I repent from self-protection, and I declare not my will but Yours in every element of my life. Holy Spirit, I invite you to come and speak to me and show me where I need to lay my plans down and pick up the plans of Heaven. Teach me to follow You and to learn Your ways. I ask that You teach me so I can be conscious of my Heavenly position and live consciously aware of who I am.

In Jesus' Name,

Amen

The clutch of purpose will dissolve the tension created by the temptation to assert our independence, releasing us to the next Gear of Grace. Empowerment.

A QUICK REVIEW

The third Gear of Grace is Authority—found through knowing your purpose.

The tension—the temptation to do things my way versus God's way.

The clutch is found in our purpose—to bring His Kingdom wherever we are.

STUDY QUESTIONS

What areas in your life have you been tempted to protect yourself from God and His plans?

Look over the desire list again. Which desires have you felt you needed to protect from God taking from you?

1. Achievement
    - Justice
    - Freedom/my way or God's way
    - Challenge/my comfort level or God's way
    - Significance/meaning
2. Connection
    - Worth in the world or Heaven's ways

- Be Known in the world or in Heaven
- Joy in my way or God's way
- Love/ my love or God's love

3. Stability
   - Belonging
   - Comfort
   - Peace
   - Security in my way or in submission

4. Competence
   - Come Through on my own strength or by God's strength
   - Goodness
   - Recognition from the world or as one who is submitted
   - Approval from the world or from God[17]

Renew - In what areas is the Holy Spirit challenging your need to protect yourself? (Remember, the renewal of our mind is learning what Heaven is saying about a thing and making that the truth we live in.)

Respond - In what ways is the Holy Spirit inviting you to trust God? (Reread the Garden of Gethsemane)

CHAPTER 6

TRANSITION

Isaiah 54:17 (NASB)
"No weapon that is formed against you will prosper."
And every tongue that accuses you in judgment you
*   will condemn.*
This is the heritage of the servants of the Lord,
And their vindication is from Me," declares the Lord.

AT THE BEGINNING OF THE LAST CHAPTER, I OBSERVED THE
potential to go at a relatively high speed in third gear. Almost enough
to go at the speed of destiny. In vehicles, there is a gauge measuring
the RPMs or revolutions per minute of the engine. It also has "the red
line," indicating the maximum RPM rate. Many Christ followers live
"revving at the redline" of any gear. They engage the clutch to relieve
the tension of the gear and coast for a moment, losing momentum.
However, because they are unwilling or don't understand how to shift
into the next gear, they return to the tension of the former gear. As
I wrote in Chapter 2, when we repent, we will return to our sin if
we don't turn from sin and turn towards the Lord. Christianity can
become very dull if we live facing tension only to lose momentum
and then simply face tension again. I don't think that is God's idea of
adventure.

The third gear of authority can feel like we are moving at the speed of destiny but can also feel like we're revving at the red line. Living in continual tension trying to discern what is or isn't God's will. Mature discipleship isn't wrestling with doing things God's way or my way.

It's found in the quiet confidence of a secure faith and established identity.

Wrestling is, however, an essential element of moving into destiny speeds because third gear establishes within us the confidence of knowing and recognizing God's will and who we are as beneficiaries of the gospel.

Before we head into the next three Gears of Grace, I will take a moment to transition us into some revelatory understandings meant for our journey through the first three gears.

FIRST REVELATORY UNDERSTANDING: TEMPTATION'S ROLE IN INTIMACY

The first revelatory understanding we need to establish is the role of temptation in our lives. The verse I quoted at the beginning of this Chapter declares that no weapon formed against us shall prosper.

Many would correctly feel that temptation is undoubtedly a weapon of the enemy that is fashioned perfectly against us. And it is. However, the promise is it won't prosper. The word also means to be profitable. Temptation is not meant to profit the enemy in any fashion. So why does he use it, and why does it seem to work?

I have said earlier that we have great authority as believers. As a result, we can only be held captive to what we choose to be held captive to. God desires our souls to prosper in absolute liberty regardless of our physical condition or circumstance.

3 John 1:2

*Beloved, I pray that in all respects **you may prosper
and be in good health, just as your soul prospers.***

As I shared earlier, to be born again is to be freeborn.

Looking back on the first three gears, you will see that a form of temptation is the cause of the tension in each gear. In first gear, it was the temptation of living in sin. The second gear's temptation was whether to choose sin or not choose sin. The third gear's temptation was to do things my way versus God's.

Take a moment and consider the results of overcoming temptation in the context of the first three gears. When temptation is overcome in each gear, it leads into the next gear. In other words, the weapon of temptation formed against you didn't prosper. Why? Because temptation led you to embrace the ways of the Kingdom of heaven. Resulting in greater intimacy with Jesus.

> *Every form
> of temptation
> is an opportu-
> nity to experience
> greater intimacy
> with Jesus.*

Every form of temptation is an opportunity to experience greater intimacy with Jesus.

This is so amazing!! We can use the very weapon of the enemy against him. He thought he could draw you away, but you used the temptation to address an inner issue, robbing you of greater intimacy, and then repented, which resulted in a whole new level of your desires being met in Jesus!!

Romans 8:28

*And we know that for those who love God, **all things
work together for good, for those who are called
according to His purpose.***

This is such a powerful promise, but one often remains unfulfilled in the lives of disciples because we do not handle temptation as a tool for us rather than a weapon against us.

SECOND REVELATORY UNDERSTANDING: DESIRE FULFILLED THE KINGDOM WAY

Psalms 16:11
You make known to me the path of life;
in Your presence, there is fullness of joy;
at Your right hand are pleasures forevermore.

In our modern Christian culture, we tend to reduce God's will to be directional, as if God's will is simply His plan for where we will be and what we will do with our lives. This way of thinking is only a partial revelation of God's will.

His will is also conditional. It's about how we will do things and who we will be in the midst of that doing.

Earlier in the book, I shared about the first level of discipleship. In our third to fourth gear experience, it becomes necessary to graduate from that first level of discipleship to another more intimate, powerful, and fulfilling connection in discipleship.

Most often, those who live most of their discipleship in the first two Gears of Grace find obedience a chore. Having been deceived into thinking that sin's answer for the desires of our hearts is better than Heaven's. Such disciples assume a posture of resistance to the nudging of the Holy Spirit. The result is a joyless, guilt-ridden, powerless religious experience. The spirit of religion depends upon our revelation of God to be limited to His acceptance of us based on our behaviour.

There is, however, another way to live as a disciple.

Proverbs 13:12
Hope deferred makes the heart sick,
but a desire fulfilled is a tree of life.

God's desire is for us to experience the fulfilment of our desires simply because He loves us, and He is good. Our commitment to the first level of discipleship shapes within us a healthy understanding of His ways as we submit to them. Submitting to His Lordship establishes the ability to respond to situations based on what we already know and have experienced in His ways. So, rather than having a crisis of faith at the corner of every temptation, we respond to temptation as a result of our knowledge and wisdom in Christ.

Psalms 37:3-5
Trust *in the Lord, and do good;*
dwell in the land and befriend faithfulness.
Delight *yourself in the Lord,*
and He will give you the desires of your heart.
Commit *your way to the Lord;*
trust in Him, and He will act.

Trust, delight, and commit. The word trust or *batah* means to have confidence and security in something. It also means to be bold about that confidence. The word delight or *anag* means to be soft or pliable. It has less to do with the excited enjoyment of delight and more with the willingness to submit, to be moldable.

The word commit, or *galal*, means to roll together, to seek occasion to trust. Today a slang term to declare how we do something is to say, "This is how we roll." Isn't it funny that we could say the same thing about this verse? It is like saying, "I roll the way He rolls."

This all ties together with the word "way." In the original language, way or *derek*, is used in the same fashion as we use the term *way* today. On the one hand, it's directional, as in, "This is the way to the grocery store." However, it also describes how something is done, like, "This is the way to tie your shoes."

There is the Kingdom way of direction and the Kingdom way of how to do things.

So, if we look at the above verse thinking about the Kingdom "how," it reads, commit your "how" to the Lord and trust Him, and He will act. And it is in our heart's commitment to the "how" of the Lord that He fulfills our desires.

At one point or another, we all have wrestled with a fork in the road decision about going in one direction or another with our lives. Most of us have sat there wondering, perhaps even worrying, about which direction was the will of the Lord for us.

> *Isaiah 30:21*
> *And your ears shall hear a word behind you, saying,*
> *"This is the way, walk in it," when you turn to the*
> *right or when you turn to the left.*

This verse illustrates that fork in the road. The word "way" here is the same as in our previous verse in Psalms 34. Isaiah writes that the reader will turn to the right *or* to the left, meaning they could choose either direction.

What if wrestling with the will of God looked a bit different? What if the voice behind you, the voice of the Lord, was revealing to you how you could walk in the ways of the Kingdom in either direction giving you the choice of the one you liked more?

> *2 Chronicles 16:9a*
> *For **the eyes of the Lord run to and fro throughout** **the whole earth, to give strong support** to those whose **heart is blameless** toward Him.*

A fully submitted heart to God becomes a safe place to dream together with the Lord strongly supporting your chosen direction.

The second level of discipleship of *desires fulfilled the Kingdom way* is a partnership between you and God. Since you have become so safe through submission to His ways, He begins to put the resources of heaven behind your ideas and desires.

> *2 Corinthians 6:*
> **Working together with Him, then, we appeal to you not to receive the grace of God in vain.**

THIRD REVELATORY UNDERSTANDING: IDENTITY FROM IMAGE AND HOLINESS

We need to simplify our struggle for identity. Truly discovering who we are will accelerate our journey into wholeness. Frankly, the greatest battle that we see in the world today is the fight to find identity. The enemy has established a frontal attack on humanity, in the realm of identity, through a worldwide religious stronghold of activity-defining identity.

People all over the world are finding their identity in what they do. Whether in marriage, career, parenthood, sexuality, recreation, or on social media, people are continually searching for affirmation of their identity by what they are doing.

Social media feeds are rampant with the heart cry of people just wanting to be noticed and affirmed. It's heartbreaking to observe people running from this to that, hoping they will be seen and loved while believing the lies. Do good, and you are good. Do something of value, and you will be valued.

God expresses His grace to humanity through identity. In the Kingdom, identity isn't earned; it is given.

And it is given in the form of an image.

Luke 20:19-26

The scribes and the chief priests sought to lay hands on Him at that very hour, for they perceived that He had told this parable against them, but they feared the people. So they watched Him and sent spies, who pretended to be sincere, that they might catch Him in something He said so as to deliver Him up to the authority and jurisdiction of the governor. So they asked Him, "Teacher, we know that You speak and teach rightly, and show no partiality, but truly teach the way of God. Is it lawful for us to give tribute to Caesar, or not?" But He perceived their craftiness, and said to them, "Show Me a denarius. Whose likeness and inscription does it have?" They said, "Caesar's." He said to them, "Then render to Caesar the things that are Caesar's, and to God the things that are God's." And they were not able in the presence of the people to catch Him in what He said, but marvelling at His answer they became silent.

I heard Daniel Colenda speak from this passage at the Azuza Street Anniversary celebration in Los Angeles. I had read this Scripture many times but from the perspective of taxes and finance, but he brought to light a perspective I had not considered before.

Jesus was giving two messages. The first was evident about paying tribute. However, the second was more of an inference that gets overlooked.

"Whose likeness and inscription does it have?" Jesus asked about the coin. But His statement asked the same question about humanity.

Whose likeness does humanity bear?

Genesis 1:26-27

God said, "Let Us make man in Our image, after Our likeness. *And let them have dominion over the fish of the sea and over the birds of the heavens and over the livestock and over all the earth and over every creeping thing that creeps on the earth."*

So God created man in His own image, in the image of God He created him; **male and female He created them.**

What is written on humanity through the covenant of the Cross?

Hebrews 10:14-16

For by a single offering he has perfected for all time those who are being sanctified.

And the Holy Spirit also bears witness to us; for after saying,

"This is the covenant that I will make with them after those days, declares the Lord:

I will put My laws on their hearts, **and write them on their minds."**

One can't find identity in activity, but in the image we bear. People will always flounder about searching for something they can do to establish their identity when the only way to find a secure identity is to enter the covenant that activates identity—the gospel.

You bear an image. The image of your Father. That image is realised by simply choosing to be grafted into the Cross, which is Heaven's Family Tree.

We can find no identity without connecting to the image we bear. And once we connect to our image maker, we explore the fullness of our identity in Him. Love, peace, security, and hope are activated within us through the power of the Cross, returning us to a conscious understanding that we possess an identity because we have found the family of our resemblance.

POWER OF DELIVERANCE

The first three Gears of Grace open us to the power of deliverance. I do not believe a demon can possess a Christian because that would entail ownership. However, I think believers can be oppressed by the demonic by establishing strongholds prohibiting people from moving beyond negative behaviours or emotions. People can be "demonized."

Strongholds are thought patterns that exalt themselves above the knowledge of Christ.

Strongholds are thought patterns that exalt themselves above the knowledge of Christ.

> *2 Corinthians 10:4-5*
> *For the weapons of our warfare are not of the flesh but have divine power to destroy strongholds. We destroy arguments and every lofty opinion raised against the knowledge of God, and take every thought captive to obey Christ.*

Through trauma, wounds, unforgiveness, sin, or simple stubborn willfulness, strongholds house the demonic, inviting their influence over our decisions and actions.

As I shared in my camp experience, the demonic realm is very real and has an absolute commitment to the destruction of people. There is no room in our lives to tolerate demonic influence or, for that matter, authority. When we accept strongholds in our lives, we agree that the demonic should be given power over us versus Jesus. This again only goes to affirm the importance of the first three Gears of Grace in overcoming temptation and establishing a value for the ways of the King and His Kingdom over our own.

Much is written on deliverance and methods that help us remove demonic influence in our lives. I am not going to affirm or debate different forms of deliverance, but for the sake of you being able to walk in freedom, I will give you some basic understanding to take hold of your freedom.

My friend Dan Baker taught me that deliverance is not a power struggle but a truth encounter. All strongholds are established through lies, and at the root of that lie is questioning God's character. When the Devil tempted Adam and Eve, he challenged God's character by telling them God was withholding from them.

> *Genesis 3:4-5*
> *But the serpent said to the woman, **"You will not surely die. For God knows that when you eat of it your eyes will be opened, and you will be like God, knowing good and evil."***

Jesus promised that we would know the truth and it would set us free, and when we are set free by Jesus, we are made freeborn. By simply accepting the truth over the lie, through repentance, we break the power of the stronghold and command the exit of the enemy. Then we invite the Holy Spirit to fill that area with the truth of Heaven and make it a positive stronghold that exalts what we know of Christ.

HOLINESS AND IMAGE BEARING

> *Romans 8:29*
> *For those whom He foreknew He also predestined **to be conformed to the image of his Son**, so that He might be the firstborn among many brothers.*

The grace message is not complete without presenting its connection with holiness. God's grace is an infinitely powerful redeeming agent of Heaven. Holiness is the beautiful result of that grace. The simplest definition of holiness is image bearing. Holiness results from believers partnering with the Holy Spirit in their image conformation. Even more simply, it's just making good decisions.

This needs to be made very clear. Holiness does not qualify you for heaven or the favour of God like the spirit of religion says it does. Holiness is not a performance; it is the result of a heart that has chosen to submit to looking like Jesus.

Jesus doesn't need a facelift. Any grace doctrine that promotes people changing the image of Jesus to suit their desires or ideologies better is false, demonic, and should be considered carnal wisdom.

James 3:13-18

*Who is wise and understanding among you? By his good conduct let him show his works in the meekness of wisdom. But if you have bitter jealousy and selfish ambition in your hearts, do not boast and be false to the truth. **This is not the wisdom that comes down from above, but is earthly, unspiritual, demonic.** For where jealousy and selfish ambition exist, **there will be disorder and every vile practice.** But the wisdom from above is first pure, then peaceable, gentle, open to reason, full of mercy and good fruits, impartial and sincere. And a harvest of righteousness is sown in peace by those who make peace.*

We must not embrace any teaching or mindset that would rob the world of experiencing the full image of Jesus.

Holiness also means consecrated or set apart. Imagine using a toothbrush as a toilet brush. Or worse, a toilet brush as a toothbrush.

Each brush is set apart for a purpose, one to clean my mouth and the other to clean my toilet. It would be profane to use them outside of their purpose. So too, it is profane for a child of God to be used outside of their purpose, which is to represent the nature of God to the world.

One of the reasons we don't understand the value of holiness is because it has been presented as our access to the acceptance of God. In other words, the more holy I am, the more God will accept me. This completely contradicts the good news of the gospel of grace. Holiness is not an activity that creates righteousness. We are made righteous through the Cross, which results in holy activities.

The spirit of religion is simply a counterfeit of holiness. While looking very much alike in outward appearance, religion operates *for* acceptance, holiness results from acceptance.

So then, rather than holiness defined as doing the right thing to be accepted by God, it becomes looking like Jesus in everything we do, which is why the description of holiness as beautiful or full of splendour in the Bible. Because holiness looks like Jesus, He is beautiful and full of splendour.

People's futile hope in finding identity and holiness in what they do manifests the simple perversion of God's ways that the enemy uses to deceive us. Holiness results from the image we bear because of our intimacy with Jesus, not the image we present because of our activities. Each of us possesses a unique design realized through the revelation of who we are in Christ. As that identity is founded, our gifts, passions, and abilities enable us to live with Kingdom purpose, which is the clutch of the third gear, bringing us to the fourth gear of grace. Empowerment.

STUDY QUESTIONS

What does the statement, "Every form of temptation is an opportunity to experience greater intimacy with Jesus" mean to you?

What mindset do you need to change to make that statement your experience?

Try to remember a time when you struggled with the directional will of God. How would that situation be different if you could view it from the perspective of the second level of discipleship of desires fulfilled?

In what ways does the thought of bearing the image of Jesus change your perspective of your identity and purpose?

How does the statement, "The spirit of religion is simply a counterfeit of holiness. While looking very much alike in outward appearance, religion operates *for* acceptance, holiness results *from* acceptance" change your perspective of holiness?

CHAPTER 7

FOURTH GEAR: EMPOWERMENT

TAKING ON YOUR TASKS

1 Corinthians 3:10

According to the grace of God given to me, like a skilled master builder I laid a foundation, and someone else is building upon it. Let each one take care how he builds upon it.

Galatians 2:9

And when James and Cephas and John, who seemed to be pillars, perceived the grace that was given to me, they gave the right hand of fellowship to Barnabas and me, that we should go to the Gentiles and they to the circumcised.

Ephesians 3:1-2

For this reason I, Paul, a prisoner for Christ Jesus on behalf of you Gentiles—assuming that you have heard of the stewardship of God's grace that was given to me for you.

THE FOURTH GEAR OF GRACE IS EMPOWERMENT.

Paul identifies that God had given him the grace to accomplish several specific tasks. We must understand that purpose will result in some form of action and responsibility God gives us.

This is the fourth gear because the previous gears work us up to destiny speed, while working those independent streaks out of us.

Now some will bristle at the thought of God giving us responsibility or work to do. Often, that independent streak robs people of experiencing true joy and peace because they choose to live outside of how the Father wired their hearts. This is the fourth gear because the previous gears work us up to destiny speed, while, at the same time, working those independent streaks out of us.

Let's create a ridiculous example to bring this point home. A six foot four, three-hundred-pound offensive lineman would not be a very successful gymnast. He might be athletic, flexible, and strong, but was created for a different sport. But what if he believed he should be a gymnast, performing flips and feats of flexibility in his floor routine? What if he is determined there is no other sport for him? He may perform the floor routine, but he was created for the football field. Perhaps even a football coach approaches him, pleading with him to try football instead, but he's convinced, he's determined, and declares his intent to continue to pursue his Olympic dreams. His independent streak results in forfeiting the millions of dollars to be made in what he was created for, and his unwillingness to see what others see robs him of the joy of real impact.

In the same way, the first three gears use sin and temptation to awaken us out of our independence, where sin tricks us into being something that we're not. Once that habit is broken, we can participate in our original design, and for our intended purpose.

He also has fashioned us perfectly and gives us grace to manage the obstacles and frustrations we might encounter while busy with His tasks.

> *Ephesians 2:10*
> *For we are His workmanship, **created** in Christ Jesus*
> *for **good works**, which God **prepared beforehand**,*
> *that we **should walk in them**.*

Consider this from the perspective of Psalm 139, where we are fearfully and wonderfully made, where God fashions us in our mother's womb, where the Father has already written a story that will give us the greatest pleasure and fulfilment for all our days, where we are completely and forever connected to His presence.

"It's a Trap"

The enemy's response is to sow the lie that God is robbing you of your choices and joy.

"Follow God," he says, "and you will lose yourself, becoming a simple-minded robot obeying God amid the miserable tasks He has given you." Satan loves to question the character of God and His goodness and sow seeds of doubt that God is primarily interested in you being miserable, always chasing but never possessing the joy promised in Scripture.

Here is the problem with that lie. It's a trap. It's the trap that leads to the cycle of searching for the will of God because we are tricked into living deactivated. The clutch of the third gear of grace is purpose, which answers the "why" of our existence. However, living with the "why" without engaging a "what" will lead to an aimless search. The fourth gear is the pursuit of the "what."

REDUCE, REFINE, RESPOND

In the third gear, I promised to share more on finding purpose or the "why" of your life.

Mark Twain said the two most important days in your life are when you are born and when you find out why.

What a wonderfully frustrating statement.

I don't know of a more confusing pursuit than purpose. God put us on the earth for a reason but finding that reason can be a lifelong frustration. We can, however, combat the frustration by simplifying the process.

REDUCE

The *Westminster Shorter Catechism* answers the question of man's chief end with this statement.

"Man's chief end is to glorify God and to enjoy Him forever."

Our first step toward the custom fit "why" of our lives is to reduce our purpose to the above statement. If you start your pursuit from this firm foundation of glorifying and enjoying God, you will begin to set the stage for more significant discoveries.

REFINE

We can focus better on how and what we are made for by glorifying God and enjoying Him as our life's default setting. This is where we can begin to refine our search based on joy.

We will engage in some things we don't enjoy, so we do them simply to glorify God, which will change our attitude and the excellence of our efforts simply because we want God to be glorified in those efforts.

However, there will be some things that we do that will give us joy. Not happiness, but joy where we find strength.

I have often quoted the Scripture from Nehemiah, saying the joy of the Lord is our strength, to celebrate God's joy strengthening us through difficult circumstances. And it's true; His joy does strengthen us.

But for fun, let's consider one other perspective.

As a parent of four great kids, I have enjoyed watching my kids excel in areas of their strengths. Whether music, art, ministry, or athletics, my kids have been a constant source of joy in my life.

What if it was the same for our Heavenly Father? What if the joy of the Lord was your strength? What if God found great joy in you, operating in your strengths?

As we reduce our purpose to glorifying God and enjoying Him, we discover areas where we serve, give, or work and find personal strengths and joy in doing them. In that refining, we get a clearer picture of our custom-made purpose, which requires a response.

RESPOND

Our response to that joy is to look for the works that God has prepared for us beforehand, according to Ephesians 2:10. This is where the grace for a task is set in motion.

Some people in my church have the grace to lead the nursery. They have the vision, passion, and a *"charis"* or joyful attitude toward babies.

I don't possess that grace. On the other hand, I do have the grace to communicate with crowds and coach them into a more profound connection with Jesus. Many don't possess that grace, and the thought of standing in front of a group of hundreds is enough to make them faint.

This illustrates what Paul was talking about in Galatians 2. He had the grace to reach out to the Gentiles, but Peter did not. Peter knew the value the Lord placed on the Gentiles but he didn't have Paul's grace to reach out to them. However, Peter did possess the grace to reach out to the Jews, which he carried out.

You and I are given an empowering grace to accomplish Kingdom assignments that God has prepared us for and prepared for us.

Now there would be many who would see my previous statement and say, "Aha! I knew it! You have been setting me up all this time to do more work for the church!"

The answer to that is a short yes but a long no.

THE SHORT YES

In short, the response to that statement is yes. There is grace given to each of us to engage in the local church's vision and mission. While some will possess the grace to lead various ministries and activities, we all will be responsible for participating in our local church's health. To connect with the church any other way is to be a consumer and expect the church to exist for your fulfilment.

I understand the busyness of life, children, activities, and creating space for family time. And leaders in the church must cast vision that makes room for those tensions felt by our families. However, at the same time, there exists a self-protective mindset amongst many in our churches, causing them to barely participate in church life except for what they might receive on a Sunday.

So, in short, yes, we need to participate in the local vision more broadly. Sadly, twenty percent of the church attendees often manage eighty percent of the church's activity. This ratio should not be the case. While this is not the purpose of this book, let me give you one tidbit of advice for managing this tension.

Determine where you and your family will participate in church and where you can't participate due to whatever restrictions. Rather than deciding that you can't participate, find where you can participate and go from there. Some tend to think that it is all or nothing, which isn't the case. It's not all, *but* it is something.

HOWEVER...

However, fourth gear isn't where we're fighting through inner turmoil due to willfulness. We dealt with those issues in first and second gear, where we learned submission and strength.

Those maturing beyond first and second gear have started to recognize the value of serving and submitting. They have started to manage authority over the enemy and steward authority in the context of their lives and leadership.

So, if willfulness is still raising its head, more than likely, you need to gear down and discover what is the cause of the independent streak and address it if you want to get up to the speed of your destiny.

THE LONG NO

Here it gets fun because we're moving into the convergence of purpose and destiny.

Unfortunately, the first thought that comes to mind when we think of God's destiny only concerns the church or missions. And sadly, business, invention, government, education, entertainment, family, creativity, and the like are left behind, as if they are not valuable to God.

God has great value for these areas, and it is confirmed by Him putting those interests, giftings, or passions in you. Again, the enemy somehow manages to convince us that the only way we can please the Lord is to be in some form of ministry while blinding us to the fact that all things are ministry to the Lord.

SACRED AND SECULAR

Exodus 35:30-33

*Then Moses said to the people of Israel, "See, the Lord has called by name Bezalel the son of Uri, son of Hur, of the tribe of Judah; and **He has filled Him with the Spirit of God, with skill, with intelligence, with knowledge, and with all craftsmanship**, to devise artistic designs, to work in gold and silver and bronze, in cutting stones for setting, and in carving wood, for work in every skilled craft.*

Bill Johnson once pointed out an essential biblical truth regarding this first mention of the infilling of the Spirit. The first infilling was upon artisans who worked with their hands (see Exodus 35:31 above). There is a principle in biblical study called "the law of first mention," which requires we consider every instance of the infilling of the Spirit through the lens of how it first happened. This means all you put your hands and hearts toward has the potential for anointing. Therefore, there is no line between sacred and secular; it is all sacred in His eyes. The world can experience the power of the Kingdom of God in every walk of life through Christ-followers.

This truth was made evident to me through the life of Garry Lefebvre, who became a hero to me. Readers in Canada will likely have heard of Circle Square Ranches. Garry was the first camp director of the first Circle Square Ranch in Halkirk, Alberta, which grew beyond Alberta to camps across Canada.

My first real experience with God was at Circle Square under Garry's leadership. But I didn't fully understand the true hero he was until a few years later when I learned that he not only founded the camp that had a huge impact on my spiritual growth but also impacted the Canadian Football League, or the CFL (Canada's professional football league), for Jesus in a powerful way.

The Grey Cup, the CFL championship game, has been one of the most-watched events in Canada for many years, but its heyday was in the 60s through the 80s. My dad and uncle were players in the CFL, and my uncle played in the 1966 Grey Cup, making the league very special to my heart.

In 1973, Garry's Edmonton Eskimos were taking on the Ottawa Rough Riders for the championship and Garry had the game of his life. He was a wide receiver, but he also served as the team's punter and, due to an injury, took over as a cornerback on defense. He scored a touchdown, had an interception as a defensive player, recovered a fumble, and kicked a punt for 85 yards. As a result, he won the Most Valuable Canadian award for the game. Sadly, it was all in vain, as the Eskimos lost to Ottawa 22-18.

What does this have to do with the joy of the Lord as your strength? In the losing effort, Garry kept a promise he made to his Bible study group. They felt that God was going to give Garry an opportunity on national TV to honor Jesus. After the loss, he accepted the award for the Most Valuable Canadian and graciously congratulated the Rough Riders. Then, he kept his promise, saying that he owed it all to Jesus because, without Him, Garry had nothing. In a later interview, he shares how he knew that God was with him that game, setting him up to keep his promise.[18]

This was one of the first times an athlete honored Jesus publicly, and after losing the championship, no less! His confession led to other players feeling confident to do the same, and it also led to a ministry to professional athletes called Athletes in Action. A simple act of giving God glory through the gift of athletics opened powerful doors for many athletes to follow.

I was blessed to get to know Garry and to thank him for the impact Circle Square had on my life and also the impact he had for Christ in the CFL and other professional leagues. His gift for athletics didn't define him; he always said he wasn't a Christian athlete but an athletic Christian. He used his strengths for the glory of God, and so can you.

Remember, the joy of the Lord is your strength. Think of it this way. Like Garry, you may have a natural strength in an area, and when you choose to use it for the glory of God, He anoints your strength. In essence, you are putting His super on your natural, making it supernatural. I have people in my church who are in construction, and they carry an anointing for it. Others are in business and possess an anointing for it; others are anointed servers, and some are anointed ministers.

The same Spirit anoints me to speak as those who build. Both bring glory to God and are a witness to the world around them.

Matthew 5:16
> *In the same way, **let your light shine before others,** so that they may see **your good works** and **give glory to your Father** who is in heaven.*

A vital truth about the Kingdom of God coming to Earth gets lost in today's version of Christianity. We are more than church services; we are more than events; we are more than sermons and social media posts.

We are the anointed ones. Christians.

The world needs anointed builders, teachers, innovators, politicians, business leaders, entertainers, sports figures, etc.

The moral decay that the world is experiencing isn't because the world has left the church but because the church has separated itself from the world.

The reduction of grace to a simple covering of sin gives space for the spirit of religion to rob the world of the revealing of children of heaven because of the sin-conscious mindset of the church. Grace reduced to sin covering alone will result in sin-focused tunnel vision.

This isn't what abundant life looks like at all. At best, it is a weak-minded, anemic version of religion which is repugnant to the world.

POINTS OF PASSION AND PROBLEMS

Not only do you have an anointing to be in any sphere of society, but you also may have a passion for or see problems outside those spheres. For some reason, things may bring tears of passion to your eyes, and you feel a tug in your heart to get involved. Or perhaps you see a problem, and it's like a pebble in your shoe, and something must be done about it.

Those things that ignite passion, or those problems that won't go away, are opportunities to step into a work God has prepared for you beforehand. The emotion or frustration attached to those passions or problems proves you have a part to play in the solution.

For example, one of my former pastors, Paul Drader, chaired our city's Drug Action Committee board. He saw the addiction problem in our community and felt the tug of God on his heart to be involved. God, through Paul, brought the mind of Christ to this problem in our city.

Paul was busy and had a family, yet God has empowered him with the grace to take leadership in our city to solve a problem.

I have another couple in my church, Rick and Manon. Both felt the pain of loss in the deaths of their first spouses to cancer. Their losses birthed within them a passion for people in the hospital. On their own, they pursued the visitation training that our health region provided so that they would be recognized as trained visitors. Their passion for the hurting has brought about a grace empowering them to love those bedridden and in need of encouragement. But it has gone beyond visitations alone. Rick will often come to me to testify about a miraculous healing or timely salvation at the bedside of the sick and dying.

These are two examples of many I could share of teachers, business-people, government workers, and labourers who allow God to operate through them in their sphere of influence and areas of passion and problems. Whether it is a civil engineer who walks in grace and anointing to solve massive, expensive city construction projects, or a schoolteacher whose love for the lost leads her and her husband into the malls to see people healed and saved. God can and will give us the grace for the task.

Fourth gear empowers us to take on the tasks the Lord has set up for us and find great fulfilment in taking them on.

MICHELLE'S STORY

My friend Michelle's story of taking on a task is beautiful.

A few years ago, I approached Pastor Landen regarding an idea I believed was a "calling" for our church. I strongly felt we needed to be more involved in our community, especially with those in need. I hoped to see a free clothing and footwear centre established and running from our church building. I believed it would bring the community to our facility and impact people spiritually and tangibly.

Pastor Landen was very supportive and encouraged me to run with the idea. While I appreciated his support, I wanted to tell him that I hadn't told him so that I would start it up but that the church should!

After we met, God began to speak to me a lot about love. While I didn't immediately see the correlation between my desire to help others and what love looks like, I know now that God was at work, strengthen-

ing and equipping me to start the clothing centre. This "work," in me, lasted for at least two years. I quit my job, knowing God asked me to make myself available during that time. Many times people would ask why I wasn't working or if I was looking for work, and my only response was, "I just want to do something that enables me to help people." Most people didn't get it, and I had no words to explain. I spent a lot of time asking God what it means to truly "love one another" and "what am I supposed to do about it?"

Later that year, during a home group meeting, we discussed our desires and passions and how we could (and should) pursue these things. I mentioned my idea about a free clothing centre. One of our friends who was part of our home group, responded with the same passion and said, "I can go buy some clothing racks, and we could do a clothing drive." We purchased racks within a week or two, and the clothing was pouring in. Our church generously provided the space and some finances and was our biggest cheerleader!

I have realized that while our church family can and should be our biggest supporters, our calling is to pursue those thoughts and ideas that won't leave us alone. We're called to dig deep into that which God has placed on our hearts while submitting the timing and results to Him. For me, trusting in God to provide and guide us in this ministry is how I learned to be in the posture of rest. So many beautiful moments have occurred at our clothing centre, from praying over the hurting to having someone come in looking for very specific sizes or items, and those items had just arrived that day.

It hasn't been easy, but that's where leaning into God's faithfulness and strength is the key. God is so faithful and will bless us as we pursue the tasks He has prepared for us. I believe it puts a smile on His face when we begin to walk out the very things He created us for because it brings us so much joy and glorifies Him!

Michelle's gifts of compassion and mercy are two of her many strengths, and her passion for seeing the church minister inside its walls and outside of them is inspiring. However, had she just left her passion in the church's hands, she wouldn't have discovered and exercised her strengths. As she said, the church should make space and support tasks taken on by its people, but it's not responsible to accomplish the tasks God gives to individuals.

There's a false sense of accomplishment when one orders their church to do something but doesn't participate in said task. It also forfeits the reward God intended for the individual with the passion for the task. When Jesus shared the parable about the talents in Matthew 25, the expectation was that the servants would *do* something with what they received. The one servant who hid his talent and did nothing had both the talent and his reward taken away.

There are 'sideline' Christians who have chosen to forfeit their opportunity to star for God's team by saying someone else should do it. Then they complain about not feeling like they have any impact or purpose.

There's no such thing as purposeless Christianity. God has placed in every person a purpose and a way for them to touch the world around them tangibly. The clothing centre that Michelle oversaw is proof of something simple, giving purpose and joy to her and, at the same time, tangibly touching our community with the generosity of God.

I also find it encouraging that Michelle's obedience to steward God's task unlocked the passion and opportunity for her friend. In essence, Michelle became the pathway for someone else to find their purpose too!

You Aren't Alone

It is important to realize that we aren't left to take on tasks alone. We have the Holy Spirit to empower us for them.

Luke 24:49

*"And behold, I am sending the promise of My Father upon you. But stay in the city until you are **clothed with power from on high**."*

ROLE OF THE HOLY SPIRIT

Acts 1:8

*"But **you will receive power** when the **Holy Spirit has come upon you**, and **you will be My witnesses in Jerusalem** and in all Judea and Samaria, and to the end of the earth."*

Before we get into the tension and clutch of fourth gear, we need to look at the role of the Holy Spirit in these last Gears of Grace. In the earlier gears, the Holy Spirit pointed out course corrections we needed to make to walk better as a disciple of Jesus. In these gears of destiny speed, the Spirit moves with us differently.

While the Holy Spirit will always aid us in our growth as image bearers, as we move forward in the gears, He anoints our gifts and obedience. As the gears unfold before us, I will expand on His role, but for now, the key is to understand that we move from being guided by the Holy Spirit to accessing the power of being filled with the Spirit.

This might not sit well with all those holding a Pentecostal doctrine of the Spirit. But I recently watched a video of Kathryn Kuhlman where she challenged her listeners not to reduce the baptism of the Holy Spirit to simply the mechanics of speaking in tongues.[19] If we are to indeed hold to a Pentecostal doctrine of the baptism of the Spirit, speaking in tongues is meant to be evidence pointing to *something greater*.

TENSION – THE SOURCE OF STRENGTH

The tension of strength becomes very real in fourth gear. Energy becomes a tangible factor in implementing the plans God would be showing us to complete. There is also the emotional toll of participating in areas of passion where your heart breaks for wholeness to be realized by those you are reaching. Or, the frustration of having to address and re-address cyclical problems. Whatever the challenge that lies before us, we begin to run out of our strength to see it through.

This tension holds so much value because it reveals to us when we are leaning into our reservoir of strength instead of accessing the power at work on our behalf.

> *Ephesians 1:18-19*
>
> *Having **the eyes of your hearts enlightened,** that you **may know** what the hope to which He has called you is, what are the riches of His glorious inheritance in the saints, and what is **the immeasurable greatness of His power toward us who believe, according to the working of His great might.***

Once we reach the end of our strength, we either quit or plug into greater power, which brings us to the first element of the Spirit's infilling.

CLOTHED WITH POWER – THE ANOINTING

> *Luke 24:48-49*
>
> *"You are witnesses of these things. And behold, I am sending the promise of My Father upon you. But **stay in the city until you are clothed with power from on high.***"

When Jesus instructed His disciples to wait on the work that He had commissioned them to do, it was so that the Holy Spirit would empower them. The first element of the Spirit's infilling is empowering us to do the work through the anointing.

Jesus modelled for us the importance of the anointing.

Luke 4:1-2

*And Jesus, **full of the Holy Spirit**, returned from the Jordan and was **led by the Spirit in the wilderness** for forty days, being tempted by the Devil. And He ate nothing during those days. And **when they were ended, He was hungry.***

Luke 4:14-15

*And Jesus **returned in the power of the Spirit** to Galilee, and a report about Him went out through all the surrounding country. And He taught in their synagogues, being glorified by all.*

Luke 4:16-21

*And He came to Nazareth, where He had been brought up. And as was His custom, **He went to the synagogue on the Sabbath day, and He stood up to read.** And the scroll of the prophet Isaiah was given to Him. He unrolled the scroll and found the place where it was written,*

*"**The Spirit of the Lord is upon Me,**
because He has anointed Me
to proclaim good news to the poor.
He has sent Me to proclaim liberty to the captives
and recovering of sight to the blind,*

to set at liberty those who are oppressed,
to proclaim the year of the Lord's favour."

And He rolled up the scroll and gave it back to the
attendant and sat down. And the eyes of all in the
synagogue were fixed on Him. And He began to say
to them, "Today this Scripture has been fulfilled in
your hearing."

As we look at the order of what happened to Jesus, we see that He was filled with the Spirit and then was led by the Spirit to the wilderness. He then returns in the power of the Spirit and declares to the listeners in the synagogue that the anointing to do the work of the Lord was His.

That same anointing is ours. The word "anointed," means to smear with oil. When your hands are covered in oil, whatever you touch ends up covered in the oil. In the same way, when the Holy Spirit has anointed you, you are the one touching them, but the Spirit is what remains on them.

The anointing causes the residue of God to be left on whatever you touch. Whether it is a sick person for healing, an idea in a meeting that brings a positive solution to an issue, a home you are building, a child you are teaching, or a patient you are nursing. Whatever you do when you are anointed leaves the touch of God.

Heaven's solutions for humanity's problems are one anointed person away from being realized.

Understanding this element of the Spirit's infilling allows us to engage the clutch fully.

CLUTCH – REST

Many would look at rest as stopping. Not so in the Kingdom. In the Kingdom of God, rest is a posture.

I often use this example to help people understand the power of rest.

In ancient Rome, they had warships called 'triremes.' The Romans filled these ships' galleys with slaves who spent their lives on the oars. But these ships also had a large mast for sails. Now imagine this ship going up a river against its current. The slaves would have to feverishly row twice as hard to combat the current to move the vessel forward. If the slaves were to stop, the current would take over and move them back downstream.

In the Kingdom of God, rest is a posture.

As believers, we are living, in a sense, against the world's current. As we journey up this river, religiously rowing, we run out of strength. Out of exhaustion, we decide to 'rest' and lift our oars, allowing the world's current to push us back downstream.

Finding the key to rest isn't in stopping but in sailing. Instead of rowing, we need to learn how to hoist the sails and use power with authority over the current, which would be the wind. In our case, we need to plug into a force that has authority over the current of the world, which is the power of God manifest through us by the anointing of the Holy Spirit.

BACK TO THE OILY HANDS

Think of it this way; when I am operating in my strength and handling something, I am touching it. When I am anointed and I touch something, God touches it. While it seems silly, which touch will likely cause a heavenly result, my touch or His?

Jack Hayford shared this powerful truth.[20] Jesus returned in the flesh after the resurrection when He spent time with His disciples. But Jesus did not shift from flesh to spirit when He ascended to heaven but stayed in the form of flesh, albeit glorified flesh. Thus ensuring humanity would be represented in the Trinity. As a result, Jesus is "firstborn among many brothers" (Rom 8:29). So then humanity is truly seated "with Him in Heavenly places" (Eph 2:6). Since Jesus is in Heaven but still in human form, He cannot be everywhere at once, so He sent the Holy Spirit.

Jesus still desires to be everywhere at once, and He has chosen to do this through the baptism of the Holy Spirit on His people so that through the resulting anointing of the baptism, Jesus, through us, can be fully present in every situation and fully powerful in those situations.

BACK TO THE RIVER AND THE TRINITY

Let's return to the ship; how do we rest, and what are the results?

To do it, we must learn the posture of rest.

WORSHIP – HOIST THE SAILS

The first aspect of rest is to activate worship. Worship is not limited to the music we experience on Sunday mornings or the albums we listen to while we drive. Worship is the natural posture of every believer. It is our privilege to live our lives as an act of worship.

Psalms 22:3
*Yet You are holy, **enthroned on the praises of Israel**.*

We can live in the Lord's presence at all times, and it is realized when we worship while we live. Teaching a class can be an act of worship. It doesn't matter if you're repairing a vehicle, policing an area, pastoring a congregation, or walking preschoolers. You are entitled to live in His presence, and the way to do it is to make every activity an act of worship.

How? Simply through thanksgiving. In all you do, be thankful to the Lord, and turn it into an act of worship. And you will have stepped into the first stage toward rest.

INTIMACY – FIND THE DIRECTION OF THE WIND

The result of worship is intimacy. We naturally draw near to Him when we choose to worship the Lord. The word for worship in Greek, "*proskyneo*," means to turn toward to kiss. The Greek word does the very best job of describing worship. One might think it is about the kiss, but it isn't. Worship is our acceptance of His invitation to intimacy.

When I invite my wife Cathy for a kiss, she turns toward me. Often at Gateway (my church in Leduc, Alberta, Canada), we say it is the turning of our attention with the intention of affection. Worship is turning our being toward God, recognizing who He is, and by the very act of turning, we engage the intimate touch of Heaven upon us.

In intimacy, we are most able to hear the voice of God and set our sails. As He speaks, He directs us to the activation of His power for any given situation.

ANOINTING – LET THE SAILS DO THEIR WORK

Now we come to the fruit of rest—the anointing working on our behalf. We have supernatural energy and power when we allow the anointing to drive our activity instead of our strength and stamina.

Yoked with Christ

Matthew 11:28-30

"Come to Me, all who labour and are heavy laden, and I will give you rest. Take My yoke upon you, and learn from Me, for I am gentle and lowly in heart, and you will find rest for your souls. For My yoke is easy, and My burden is light."

Jesus promises us that we find rest when we are in His yoke. So, what is His yoke? There is a reality to this empowerment that many do not experience because of our limited view of the gospel.

The gospel covenant isn't limited to the message of salvation. It also includes the invitation to be fastened to Christ. The yoke that Jesus offered was freedom from the religious oppression that had become the Pharisaical laws. His offer remains today; however, being yoked to Him brings us to a truth we don't often experience.

If Cathy and I adopted a little girl, we would bring her into our relationship. She would experience our love and happiness; she would be secure as we are. In other words, she would experience us. In the same way, when we come into a saving knowledge of Jesus, we are brought into His relationship—the relationship of the Trinity.

John 17:21

*"That they may all be one, just as You, Father, are in Me, and I in You, **that they also may be in Us**, so that the world may believe that You have sent Me."*

The gospel brings us into a relationship *with* the Trinity but also sets us into the relationship *of* the Trinity. That is why when Jesus said He would give His peace or His joy, He was referring to the peace and joy that is the experience of the Trinity. Like the little girl would experience the security of my love with Cathy, we get to experience the Trinity's love, peace, joy, strength, and power.

With this in mind, our perspective of peace changes, and we understand why it is a peace that passes understanding because it is part of the infinite divine dance of the Trinity. We now can understand why it is life abundantly because it is the life of the Trinity. It's why joy can be complete, because of the fullness of joy of the Trinity.

Rather than trying to muster up some form of superhuman peace or love or joy, all we need to do is ask the Holy Spirit to open the eyes of our hearts to see the immeasurable power that is a work on behalf of us who believe.

CLUTCH PRAYER – REPENT

Jesus, I thank You for empowering me with grace for works. I repent of doing things in my strength, and please teach me how to live at rest. Thank You for the power at work on my behalf, and I invite You to fill my sails with your anointing to accomplish what you have set before me. I ask for a fresh encounter with Your goodness and that I would experience the peace and joy of the Trinity today.

In Jesus' Name,

Amen

A QUICK REVIEW

The fourth gear of grace is Empowerment: taking on your tasks.

The tension is the source of strength.

The clutch is rest—hoist the sails, worship.

Find the direction of the wind, which is intimacy.

Let the sails do the work, which is the Spirit's anointing.

The clutch of rest prepares us to move into the next two gears of grace. Sustaining Grace and Radical Obedience.

STUDY QUESTIONS

In what ways have you believed that engaging in a task from God would make you miserable?

What changes in your thinking when you consider that God would give you things to do, that would cause you to be fulfilled?

How does the thought that everything you do is sacred, shift your attitude toward your daily activities?

In light of the statement, "Those things that ignite passion, or those problems that won't go away, are opportunities to step into a work that God has previously prepared for you. The emotion or frustration attached to those passions or problems prove you have a part to play in the solution." What are some of those areas of passion in your life that you perhaps have just brushed off and not engaged in? What is God inviting you to do about it?

Renew - In what ways is the Holy Spirit challenging you to reconsider your purpose? (Remember, the renewal of our mind is learning what Heaven is saying about a thing and making that the truth we live in.)

Respond - In what areas does God anoint you to walk in power? In what ways do you feel you are being invited to take the risk to walk in greater anointing? (Reread the Clothed With Power section)

CHAPTER 8

Fifth Gear: Sustaining Grace

Grace to Wander the Wilderness

Song of Solomon 8:5a
Who is that coming up from the wilderness, leaning on her beloved?

THE FIFTH GEAR OF GRACE IS SUSTAINING GRACE.

What do you do when it feels like your prayers are unanswered? When it seems like Heaven has said, "Wait"? Or worse, "No"?

What do you do when you feel abandoned, alone, wandering through the wilderness of doubt, confusion, pain, suffering, and loss?

How do we manage our hearts when all four core questions, "Am I accepted" "Am I valued" "Am I able" and "Do I matter," are being challenged to our very depths?

Managing disappointment, heartbreak, and drought of the soul is real and can have glorious or devastating results for Christ followers. Some will come out of wilderness experiences *leaning on their beloved,* as the Scripture says above, others will reject Him.

2 Corinthians 12:7-10

So to keep me from becoming conceited because of the surpassing greatness of the revelations, a thorn was given me in the flesh, a messenger of Satan to harass me, to keep me from becoming conceited. Three times I pleaded with the Lord about this, that it should leave me. But He said to me, "My grace is sufficient for you, for My power is made perfect in weakness." Therefore, I will boast all the more gladly of my weaknesses, so that the power of Christ may rest upon me. For the sake of Christ, then, I am content with weaknesses, insults, hardships, persecutions, and calamities. For when I am weak, then I am strong.

Many scholars have debated what this "thorn in the flesh" that Paul was lamenting was. Some from curiosity, others in the hope that in discovering his trial, we would gain insight into overcoming trials. In fact, Paul gives us the secret to overcoming through Jesus' answer to his prayer.

"My grace is enough."

Sustaining grace is the supernatural strength to steward journeys through the wilderness.

To help us navigate this Chapter, I will identify two categories of wildernesses. We will refer to one as storms and the other as deserts. Both wildernesses will have similarities, but there will also be some vast differences. The primary difference will be their source.

"Why and When?" or "What and How?"

Most of us in the throes of trial, or the painful length of the process, ask the wrong questions. In so doing, we set ourselves up for frustration and anger. We naturally want to know why it is happening and when it will be over.

"Why" isn't a forbidden question, just often a poorly timed one. "Why" is often a question that finds its answer at the end of the trial. Imagine you were in day surgery, and the surgeon was doing a minor surgery while you were awake and aware. If you were to ask the surgeon why each cut was happening or the reason for each probe and stitch, you would prolong the surgery. In the same way, asking when it will be over with each move of the surgeon's scalpel would likely result in the answer, "When it's done."

We don't challenge God's patience by asking why, nor test His capacity for completion with "when." But our acceptance of His character and our maturity are being challenged.

GOD IS GOOD

In my book *Renovated for Glory*, I examine the goodness of God in detail, but we must discuss it here because a lengthy trial or process challenges our perception of His goodness. And He rises to that challenge.

At Bethel Church in Redding, California, Pastor Bill Johnson has beautifully brought God's goodness to light in recent years. As I have shared earlier, the promise that no weapon formed against us shall prosper (Isa 54:17) points to the goodness of God.

God doesn't do bad things to people to teach them a lesson. He doesn't make you sick, so He can make you better or teach you something.

Hebrews 1:1-3

Long ago, at many times and in many ways, God spoke to our fathers by the prophets, but in these last days He has spoken to us by his Son, whom He (the Father)

appointed the heir of all things, through Whom also
He created the world. He (Jesus) is the radiance of
the glory of God and the exact imprint of His (the
Father's) nature.

Jesus is the perfect representation of the nature of His Father. If you don't see it in Jesus, it doesn't exist in the Father.

Jesus didn't go around making people sick so that He could make them better. He didn't lean down to the blind person and say, "God is trying to teach you something." He just healed them. He didn't tell the lame, "You deserve this because of your sin." He just healed them. He didn't say to the leper, "Don't come near me; you're unclean!" He touched them and then made them clean.

Why tell you this? Because the job description of the enemy is to steal, kill and destroy, but Jesus' is to bring life and life abundantly.

John 10:10
The thief comes only to steal and kill and destroy. I
came that they may have life and have it abundantly.

If it looks like steal, kill, or destroy, its genesis isn't in the Father; it is from the enemy. I no longer look to the heavens asking why something destructive is happening. I know whose job description is whose.

But we are not left without hope because no weapon formed against us shall prosper.

Romans 8:28
*And we know that for those who love God, **all things***
work together for good,** for those who are **called
according to His purpose.

This is how no weapon prospers against us. God uses whatever the enemy throws at us for our good, growth, inner health, and future.

And in the turmoil, the pain, the loss, and the frustration, we can garner strength knowing that He has the future well in hand but gives us the promise that His grace is enough for us to navigate through the stormy seas of discontent.

This is why this gear or revelation of God's grace is vital. We need this grace to survive these wilderness seasons, and it helps us ask the right questions, which are "What and How?"

"WHAT ARE YOU DOING IN ME?"

"God's trying to…" I hear this as a start to a statement about what God is doing or saying a lot as a pastor. And in truth, I have said it myself. But I have since tried to remove that prefix from any thoughts about God. The reason is that it is a wrong statement. God doesn't *try* to do anything. He does it. We are the ones who are trying to hear, learn, grow, embrace, and implement what God is saying or doing.

I share this because when we think God is trying, we suggest that the wilderness has more authority than our Father. This isn't true, but it is a subtle lie sown by the enemy to put our faith on the defensive. It also creates space for doubt to become the lens through which we view our processes.

A great question to ask Him in our wilderness seasons is, "What are You doing in me?" Not *to* me but *in* me. What are You refining? What mindset are You shifting/developing? How are You renewing the way I think, see, or hear?

The next question is, "How do I respond?"

Isaiah 64:8

But now, O Lord, You are our Father;
we are the clay, and You are our potter;
we are all the work of Your hand.

We have the choice to react or respond to the potter's hands. Scripture admonishes the foolishness of the clay's assumptions about the potter.

Isaiah 29:16

You turn things upside down!
Shall the potter be regarded as the clay, that the
thing made should say of its maker, "He did not
make me"; or the thing formed, say of Him who
formed it, "He has no understanding?"

Even so, as children with the gift of self-determination through our free will, we still have the choice to react or respond to the potter's hand.

Our fleshly urges will always try to protect themselves, and a reaction is a defensive posture to outside stimuli. Think of how you blink when something flashes in front of your face. Your eyelids react to that stimulus by trying to protect your eyes. I remember contests as a kid trying not to blink when friends would flash their hands in front of my face to see which of us had nerves of steel. I remember the self-control it took not to blink.

In the same way, we can exercise the spiritual gift of self-control not to react to God's hand but rather to respond to Him by submitting to His hand, reshaping what the enemy has tried to destroy.

Here is where the power of sustaining grace is manifest. When we respond in the fashion that God encourages us to, we access sustaining grace that strengthens us to endure. Said another way, on the other side of our obedience to His direction is the grace that will calm our fears, ease our pain and bring rest, even during the storm. It might not calm storms, but it will calm nerves.

> *Luke 8:22-25*
>
> *One day, He got into a boat with His disciples, and He said to them, "Let us go across to the other side of the lake." So they set out, and as they sailed, He fell asleep. And a windstorm came down on the lake, and they were filling with water and were in danger. And they went and woke Him, saying, "Master, Master, we are perishing!" And He awoke and rebuked the wind and the raging waves, and they ceased, and there was a calm. He said to them, "Where is your faith?" And they were afraid, and they marvelled, saying to one another, "Who then is this, that He commands even winds and water, and they obey Him?"*

We will examine two instances of this truth Jesus let the disciples experience.

First, in the Scripture I just shared from Luke, Jesus told the disciples that He wanted to go to the other side of the lake. He gets in the boat, and they cast off. This massive storm comes up, and it is a severe storm. Don't forget He had some fishermen who had spent their lives on the water and even they were afraid. These weren't rookies at dealing with the weather. It must have been severe.

Even so, Jesus, a carpenter, not a seaman, is asleep. Why?

Because He said they were going to the other side. If Jesus says to do something and you obey, no storm of hell can stop it from happening, and you can be at peace. He asked them about their faith, and the question behind it was, was their faith in what they were seeing or experiencing or that He was with them? Let's look at the second lesson.

Mark 6:45-51

Immediately, He made His disciples get into the boat and go before Him to the other side, to Bethsaida, while He dismissed the crowd. *And after He had taken leave of them, He went up on the mountain to pray. And when evening came, the boat was out on the sea, and He was alone on the land. And He saw that they were making headway painfully, for the wind was against them.* **And about the fourth watch of the night He came to them, walking on the sea.** *He meant to pass by them, but when they saw Him walking on the sea, they thought it was a ghost, and cried out, for they all saw Him and were terrified. But immediately He spoke to them and said, "Take heart; it is I. Do not be afraid." And He got into the boat with them, and the wind ceased. And they were utterly astounded.*

Second, another boat ride, another challenge, this time straining against an opposing wind. So, Jesus decides to walk out on the water, impressive enough to be sure, but He intends to walk past them. Two things jump out to me. The first is that if Jesus says He's going to meet you on the other side, no wind, no opposition, and no devil in hell will stop that. But secondly, He gets into the boat and calms the wind.

This, for me, is a picture of sustaining grace. We can follow Him, and He gives us the choice. Jesus will meet us on the other side because He told us to go there, which means He will provide the strength to get there, or we can call on Jesus, and He will calm the influence of the opposition on us. It's called peace that surpasses understanding. No rebuke this time, just an encouragement that He's there and you don't have to fear.

TANGIE'S STORY

In 2 Corinthians 12:9, it says, "And he said unto me, My grace is sufficient for thee; for my strength is made perfect in weakness. Most gladly, therefore, will I rather glory in my infirmities, that the power of Christ may rest upon me"

We are familiar with this scripture, or at least the first part of it. We often see the long journeys through stormy waters as punishment, leaving us feeling abandoned, disregarded, or discarded by God. But this scripture redirects our thoughts to something bigger – the power of God manifested in our lives through the storm. Long-suffering is something no one is prepared for and, through its duration, constantly tests faith. For 24 years, my husband suffered from ongoing health issues that would eventually require a liver transplant. Over 16 of those years, his diagnosis of PSC wreaked havoc on his body and caused other damage. We call those damages the "leftovers." There were open sores on his legs that wouldn't heal, requiring constant attention to avoid infection, and severe ulcerative cholangitis. He also fought through C-difficile and Colitis leaving him a prisoner in his own home.

We were a young family, and Jason could no longer work. It stripped away his identity, and our future changed forever. Our hopes and dreams to grow old together hung in the balance.

There was no cure except a liver transplant.

So we moved from Saskatchewan to Alberta to live with my parents. Which allowed to be closer to the doctors who kept tabs on the disease and its progression.

My parents were able to help with our children, and I was able to go back to work to help with our finances and debts that accumulated over time. After some time, we moved into my parent's rental property and started to build a "home." Then in 2012, I lost my job, and I really didn't know what to do next; with that, Jason's health began to decline rapidly, and I provided the full-time care he needed. His health declined leaving him in a wheelchair, and he needed to visit the hospital daily for wound care, tests, procedures, physiotherapy, and home care.

We had many close calls over the next three years, and one night the ambulances came taking him to the hospital where he would stay until he received a transplant or didn't. I spent every day at the hospital for eight months.

I received a phone call the morning before Mother's Day. Jay was in the ICU, and they weren't confident he'd live through the next 24hrs. As I sat in a little room by myself down the hall from where they were trying to save Jason's life, I began to cry out, "I don't know what to do, God; I don't know what to do!"

In this darkest moment, when it seemed hopeless, I remembered the powerful grace of God that sustained us throughout the storm. The last paragraph may have left you wondering where God was in all this. Where was He?

This is a short version of our story, and if we only told this story of doom and gloom and "camped out" there, it would be a sad story. However, years of God's faithfulness through the storm, in our darkest moments, and during times of great need are also part of our story.

At every turn, He carried us, and our lives are FULL of testimonies of God's faithfulness. I don't deny the profound hurt, pain, and suffering. It was and is very real, but His power that continued to operate through us and in us during this trial and our ongoing trial is undeniable. We have seen the miracles of God.

For four years, Jason lived under a misdiagnosis, but we pressed in and asked God to help us find out what was wrong, and He answered. Did it happen right away? No, but God answered. We asked over and over again for His strength to carry us, and He answered, giving us glimpses every day that He was with us. We asked for groceries and food for our table. And He answered with people showing up at our door with everything written on my grocery list hanging on the fridge. Even the extra things I had crossed off the list thinking they were not necessities, but He felt we should have them anyway. We asked for gas to get to doctors' appointments and got gas gift cards in the mail.

Jason found a new identity when he couldn't work to replace what was stripped away. He became a "Superhero dad," spending every moment with our children – and it was such a blessing! When my heart ached, and I didn't think I could handle it, God answered and lent me His strength. When Jason's body was failing him, God did not fail him, and he gave him strength for each day.

When we had to move in with my parents, our children received loads of grandparent time and built memories that would be with them forever. When I lost my job, and it was time to take care of bigger things, namely Jason, opportunities for me to pour into ministries in the areas of my passion, like building an art ministry, running Gateway's women's ministry, and teaching art.

In all this, I felt filled by His Spirit, not empty or exhausted.

When we were in the hospital indefinitely until a transplant, we had nurses and doctors stopping in our room on their breaks just to chat, and we were able to share the grace and strength of God, and they saw it tangibly operating in our lives even through the storm. We saw God give Jason back his life over and over. In truth, the testimony of God's grace over our lives could fill a book. We don't always understand the why behind the journey, and I have come to accept that I may not ever know the why, but without this journey, we would also be void of the testimony.

But let me finish the story and add in God's sustaining grace.

As I sat in that little room by myself down the hall from where they were trying to save Jason's life, I began to cry out, "I don't know what to do, God; I don't know what to do!" I then remembered from all the years of training, "I know what to do," I fell to my knees and gave this situation like so many before back to HIM and asked Him for His strength. At that moment, His great grace fell, and a peace beyond understanding covered me. I knew He was in control, and nothing was in my control. I gave it all to Him at that moment, and my heart was ready to receive whatever was next. Regardless of everything that happened next, I knew He would care for us.

When Jay stabilized, I was able to go into the room. There were machines and tubes everywhere, and I looked at my husband, 100% on life support. But I also saw three angels beside the nurses working in the room.

I stopped, and as I considered Jay's condition, I quickly asked the Lord, "Is it time, God...is it time to let Jay go?"

I heard a small whisper I had become familiar with throughout our storms that said, "Not yet."

That's all I needed to hear. The grace of God covered me, and He lent me His strength as I had no more. I walked over to Jason and whispered in his ear, "Get in the fight, babe. You're not done yet!"

The next day Jason went from 100% life support to 75% and was awake. They told me he wouldn't remember a lot of things at first. But not my Jay; he wrote on a piece of paper, "Happy Mother's Day!" Truly the best gift ever! But he wasn't done. He wrote down the nurses' names who helped him before going into ICU and asked if they were ok. And, of course, he wanted to know who won the hockey game.

The following night I got a call at 2 am from ICU, and I answered quickly, wondering what would have happened now, and the staff there told me Jason was off life support!

When I arrived at the hospital that morning, the nurses jumped and cheered, saying, "You don't understand Tangie, this doesn't happen! It's a miracle!"

Jason's progress was undeniably a miracle.

Two weeks later, we got the news that Jason would receive a transplant, which saved his life. We have spent the last six years since that day rejoicing to have him here with us.

Is there still a journey left? Yes. Are we still being challenged and waiting on the fulfilment of promises? Yes. Are we still dealing with some "leftovers?" Yes. But it has been God's sustaining grace that lends us strength.

As you consider our story of God's sustaining Grace, there are a few thoughts we'd like to leave with you that we now live by:

1. *Never allow circumstances to dictate how you respond to God or prohibit you from what He asks you to do. Look for God's blessings each day and thank Him. A heart of thankfulness that sees His blessings doesn't allow the circumstances to overshadow you. Storms don't get to steal your call. Ask Him how to engage your call on your life, even during the storm.*

2. *ASK for his strength, invite Him into your storm, and give every circumstance to Him, even if it means 100 times a day for 24 years. He covers you with grace and lends you His strength.*

3. *He never gives up on you, so don't give up on Him. You can rely on the character of God because He is who He says He is. God is Good. He is not punishing you. We live in a fallen world, and because of that, we can be subject to the fallen things that happen in it. But because of Jesus, we are not of this world, which means*

*we have access to something more significant to carry us. That
makes us look different from the rest of the world, including how
we weather the storm.*

4. *Press into God. Don't push Him away even when you don't
   understand. Remember that through all the mess and pain, He
   loves you, and with Him, you can overcome.*

*"My strength is made perfect in weakness," or as I like to say, when I
am weak, He is strong in me and for me.*

*I will leave you with this last familiar scripture, and maybe it will
help you see it in a different light now.*

Is. 40:3

*"But they that wait upon the Lord shall renew their
strength; they shall mount up with wings as eagles, they
shall run and not be weary; they shall walk and not
faint"*

TENSION – GO BACK TO EGYPT!

The tension of this gear, and let's face it, this gear is *all* tension, is
to relinquish your authority and return to old slavers waiting for you
in the first and second gears. The enemy plans to trick us into giving
up our authority by making circumstances the focus of attention to
deceive us into returning to bondage.

The children of Israel almost fell for this trick in the wilderness.

Numbers 11:5

**We remember the fish we ate
in Egypt that cost nothing, the
cucumbers, the melons, the leeks,
the onions, and the garlic.**

*and let's face
it, this gear is
all tension,*

They remembered the things that satiated their appetites, comforted them, and how there was no cost. All the while forgetting that while they were in Egypt, they were slaves.

Can you see the parallel to our lives when we are going through the wilderness? Earlier in our journey, I shared the four questions we need answered by the love of God that the enemy tries to trick us into satiating through sin.

How is it so easy to forget former slavery? How is it so easy to disregard freedom from sin and fall into temptation? For that answer, we must return to the garden we discussed in second gear, the Management of Liberty.

As you will remember, earlier, we discussed the lie the enemy used to deceive Adam and Eve of their authority; which was to question the character of God. In their case, he accused God of withholding from Adam and Eve. In the second gear, the management of liberty, Satan questions God's character by accusing Him of not being good.

When the pressures of the wilderness bear down on us, the Accuser deflects blame from himself and points at God as the author of our troubles. And then he has the nerve to accuse God of not being good to us. Then he sets before us whatever sin will satiate, give a fix, or temporarily numb us to the pain he has caused.

His goal? To steal your authority, just like he did to Adam and Eve. And just like he tried to do to Jesus.

When Satan tempted Jesus, he revealed that he had that authority and was willing to give it to Jesus if Jesus would worship him.

Luke 4:5-7
*And the Devil took Him up and showed Him all the Kingdoms of the world in a moment of time, and said to Him, "To you **I will give all this authority** and*

> *their glory, for **it has been delivered to me, and I give it to whom I will. If You, then, will worship me, it will all be Yours.***"*

And he tries to tempt us the same way. He is trying to convince us to give over our authority to him.

Earlier in second gear, you learned how to use strength, the inner resolve to overcome, to win over temptation, and reflect your true identity in Christ by consistently leaning toward your perfection rather than imperfection. This gave you access to authority, which turned you into a threat.

In the same way, Satan attempted to deceive Jesus, focusing on His present weakness and hunger because of His forty-day fast. Satan's plan was to take Jesus' focus off of the purpose for which He came. And like you and I are now able, Jesus engaged the clutch of third gear, purpose, and He overcame. Jesus then fulfilled His purpose through the Cross and His resurrection, and now we can overcome too!

Satan couldn't see the end game of the Cross but prepared to hunker down for the long game. He knew Jesus on the earth meant trouble was brewing, but he couldn't decode God's plan for all of humanity's redemption. So, in trying to trick Jesus out of His authority, the enemy was willing to give up his control over the earth for the span of Jesus' life. Jesus, however, knew the plan of His Father wasn't short term, but eternal.

Similarly, when we relinquish our authority, we may experience temporal reprieve, but eternal purposes are lost, which robs us of our purpose and destiny, holding us back from destiny speed. But what if there is a pathway?

What if God Brings You to the Wilderness?

I have said that God is good. I stand by that. I have also noted that the enemy is the author of negative things in our lives. I stand by that. But we must also consider that the Bible says God can call us into the wilderness. Even trick us into going there.

Here is where I would like to identify the two wildernesses I referred to earlier. The first, we will call storms. The second we will call deserts. One comes from the enemy, the other from the Lord.

Storms are sudden surprise sideswipes the enemy uses to bring destruction and steal from our lives. However, deserts are dry seasons of the soul. The enemy will cause the odd storm in a desert, but deserts differ from storms because of our invitation to them.

Hosea 2:14-15
"Therefore, behold, I will allure her,
and bring her into the wilderness,
and speak tenderly to her."

Here He is saying that He will draw us into wilderness moments. He even led Jesus to the wilderness.

Luke 4:1-2
*And Jesus, full of the Holy Spirit, returned from the Jordan and **was led by the Spirit in the wilderness** for forty days, being tempted by the Devil. And He ate nothing during those days. **And when they were ended, He was hungry.***

Why?

To speak tenderly, to show us love we didn't know we could have. To teach us how to overcome when we are weak. The first Scripture I shared at the beginning of this Chapter was Song of Solomon 8:5.

Solomon 8:5

*Who is that coming up from the wilderness, **leaning on her beloved?***

Leaning on her beloved. Not standing alone in her own great strength, not a force to be reckoned with on her own, but leaning on, intimate, dependent, strengthened by, filled with, and totally surrendered to her beloved, Jesus.

But the enemy will try, even in a desert that God has brought us into, to steal, kill and destroy. Satan will try to send storms to abort God's work within us in the desert. But what happens in the desert is that God is refining, pruning, and starving things out of us and preparing us for the promises ahead.

When the children of Israel went into the desert, their wandering revealed their slave mindset. God chose Moses to lead them because he wasn't enslaved even though he was a Hebrew. He grew up a prince. A prince thinks differently than a slave. The slave's mindset will never be able to manage the promises of God. In the case of Israel's children, that generation of slaves couldn't inherit the Promised Land.

In like manner, our deserts starve out the slave mindsets that rob us from moving into our promised lands. Those areas in our lives where we still think from the influence of our old nature. Those areas where the enemy tricks us into believing that something other than the love of God can fulfill our desires.

John 15:1-2

"I am the true vine, and My Father is the vine-dresser. Every branch in Me that does not bear fruit He takes

away, **and every branch that does bear fruit He
prunes,** *that it may bear more fruit."*

Deserts are God's way of pruning us, cutting away the things that
are stealing our potential for fruit and more fruit. Earlier, I shared how
God is a gardener. Good gardeners know what needs to be cut back so
more fruit will grow. My wife and I have an apple tree in our backyard.
She likes it to look a certain way but wants it to bear fruit. The problem
is that the long branches take up the nutrients that cause the fruit to
grow, leaving us with marginal fruit. But when we cut those branches
back, the tree doesn't look as impressive, but its fruit is terrific.

Likewise, in our lives, how we look occasionally affects how we
produce. We like to present ourselves as solid and mighty trees, but
that doesn't impress our Father. He is impressed by fruit-bearing. So,
God invites us into a desert season to prune, refine, and starve the
branches, mindsets, attitudes, and activities to grow the fruit.

This fifth gear of sustaining grace is where we can become very
fruitful. Whether it is a desert or a storm, the good news is that it all
continues to work together for our good. The desert is designed to
cause fruitfulness, and and God can use the enemy's storms to do
likewise. Either way, we are destined to bear greater fruit in this gear.
I can't stress this enough, every event, whether stormy or dry, can be
used by God to bring you into a deeper relationship with Him.

Every single one.

I'm sharing this to encourage you. Storms and deserts don't reflect
God's negative view of your life. They are not your fault, and God, in
His great love for you, will not let any weapon prosper over you, and at
the end of the desert, He has a promise waiting for you.

Storms and deserts will change you .

YOUR WRESTLING MATCH

Genesis 32:24-25

And Jacob was left alone. And a man wrestled with him until the breaking of the day. When the man saw that he did not prevail against Jacob, he touched his hip socket, and Jacob's hip was put out of joint as he wrestled with him.

Each of us needs to have our wrestle with God, and He doesn't fight dirty, just in His way. He won't prevail upon us to simply overcome us; He will prevail by bringing brokenness that leads to dependence. This is why we come out of the wilderness, leaning on our beloved.

Genesis 32:30-31

So Jacob called the name of the place Peniel, saying, "For I have seen God face to face, and yet my life has been delivered." The sun rose upon him as he passed Penuel, limping because of his hip.

I have a great friend named Trevor, who once told me that his dad always said, "Never trust a man without a limp."

Profound advice.

The Bible gives no evidence that Jacob's hip was ever healed of the limp. This means he limped into every battle and away from every victory, dependent on His God.

But how do we discern the difference between a storm and a desert? By how they start. Storms are always surprise attacks. They come out of nowhere. However, deserts begin with an invitation by God, and then He plays Laban.

What do I mean by that? I will share that in a moment.

CLUTCH – FAITHFULNESS

Psalms 119:30
**I have chosen the way of faithfulness;
I set Your rules before me.**

The clutch for this gear is faithfulness. Regardless of whether you
are in a storm or desert, faithfulness
brings fruitfulness. This means you
can bear great fruit even in your desert
or storm.

*Regardless of
whether you are in
a storm or desert,
faithfulness brings
fruitfulness.*

What makes sustaining grace so
unique is its miraculous speed.

In any average vehicle, when you
reach the end of a gear's potential, as I shared at the beginning of the
book, you engage the clutch, and for a moment, you coast on your
momentum and then shift it into the next gear.

If you were to just leave in the clutch, your momentum begins to
fade, and you find yourself going too slow to shift into the next gear.

Not so with sustaining grace. This makes it phenomenal, and
why we must go through it. You don't lose speed when you engage the
clutch of faithfulness and coast. In fact, in some ways, you gain speed.

There was a delay in publishing this book. I thought it was
resistance, but then the Lord clarified that it was because this Chapter
had to be written and added. Because so many believers find themselves
in a prolonged desert or storm and feel like they have hit their ceiling
in their fruitfulness and purpose and that perhaps destiny has been
robbed from them.

Faithfulness postures us for greater fruitfulness even during these wilderness seasons. It prepares us to walk in greater intimacy with Him and with clarity from Him.

My wife went through a painful back issue several years ago that left her bedridden in tremendous pain for several months. Our four kids were under ten at the time, and the house had to continue functioning. It was a trying time, especially for Cathy.

She lay in our room crying because of the pain; I couldn't help. I felt helpless, she felt hopeless, and our kids still needed us.

We would have been destroyed had it not been for faithfulness.

My wife would lean into Jesus. We would watch programs on healing and encourage our souls. She began to meet with Jesus in ways that made me jealous, and on the night before she was having surgery for her back, we were praying, and she prayed, "Jesus, if I risk losing the love I am experiencing with you by getting better, I'd rather stay sick."

She had engaged sustaining grace.

This miraculous strength to continue leads to miraculous fruit bearing. For some, the storm becomes a new normal; for others, it is an intense short battle of their life. Regardless of length or intensity, it does not rob you of continuing to move forward at the speed of destiny because it becomes the practice field for the posture of rest necessary in future gears.

But the desert also bears some other unique fruit that prepares us for the promised land.

FROM SLAVES TO SOLDIERS

Exodus 15:16
Terror and dread fall upon them;

>*because of the greatness of Your arm, they are still*
>>*as a stone,*
>*till Your people, O Lord, pass by,*
>*till the people pass by whom You have purchased.*

Israel left Egypt a ragtag group of slaves. But they entered Canaan as a fighting force to be feared. The desert had prepared them for the promise.

It can do the same for you.

WHEN GOD PLAYS LABAN

Years ago, at the Pensacola revival, I heard John Kilpatrick preach what I am about to share, and it became my life message.

In Genesis 29, Jacob speaks with some servants near a well. And then this beautiful woman walks up. Her name is Rachel. And Jacob sees her and falls in love.

She introduces him to her dad, Laban, and Jacob offers to serve Laban for seven years to have Rachel's hand in marriage. Laban agrees.

>*Genesis 29:20-21*
>*So Jacob served seven years for Rachel, and they seemed to him but a few days because of his love for her. Then Jacob said to Laban, "Give me my wife that I may go into her, for my time is completed."*

So, the seven years are complete, and they went by like a few days because of Jacob's great love for Rachel. But then he says, "Give me my wife that I may go into her." Jacob had waited long enough; he was ready to have his wife.

Now this is important; he was speaking of sleeping with her. There was some lust in the equation here. I will expand on that in a moment.

So, Laban prepares the wedding. But then he does something that catches Jacob off guard.

> *Genesis 29:22-25*
>
> *So Laban gathered together all the people of the place and made a feast. But in the evening he took his daughter Leah and brought her to Jacob, and he went into her. (Laban gave his female servant Zilpah to his daughter Leah to be her servant.)* **And in the morning, behold, it was Leah! And Jacob said to Laban, "What is this you have done to me? Did I not serve with you for Rachel? Why then have you deceived me?"**

Behold, it was Leah!

Now I've heard about being drunk on love, but they must've partied pretty hard for Jacob not to have any sense of who he was sleeping with!

You see, Rachel had an older sister, Leah. The Bible says she had weak eyes and lacked beauty compared to Rachel.

Jacob has a legitimate beef with Laban; after all, he has spent seven years serving him for Rachel, not Leah.

Laban's response is fascinating.

> *Genesis 29:26-28*
>
> *Laban said,* **"It is not so done in our country, to give the younger before the firstborn.** *Complete the week of this one, and we will give you the other also in return for serving me another seven years." Jacob did so and completed her week. Then Laban gave him his daughter Rachel to be his wife.*

Let's bring the story to our context.

God didn't tell the children of Israel about the desert; he told them about the Promised Land. Laban didn't tell Jacob about Leah. He told him about Rachel.

God is not dumb. He knows that if He were to come to you and say, "I have this amazing desert for you, there will be storms, dry places, confusion, and doubt. While there, I will likely crush you into powder. But take heart, when it's over, and you won't know when I will determine it is over, you will have a promise that I'll show you then."

Not very many sane people would take Him up on that offer. Most would say, "Not me, thanks. I'll stay in Egypt!"

But He doesn't do that. He shows us the land flowing with milk and honey; He shows us the promise, the beautiful, voluptuous, intoxicating Rachel.

And with a glassy-eyed, dumbstruck look, we say, "I'll serve you for seven years!"

He invites us, and we say, "YES!"

It sort of goes down like this. You're at the altar after a powerful, inspiring message feeling the call of God into your destiny. Into your purpose. Into the promise of God over your life. As you are there, likely weeping in both joy and anticipation, someone comes along and prophesies that you will go to the nations, that you will write, that you will have a TV ministry, that you will never lack provision, and that you will change the world.

And drunk with love, we pray the prayer, the dangerous prayer, the foolish prayer, that God will always answer!

"Whatever you need to do in me, Lord. Go ahead, do it! I give you permission; You are the Potter, I am the clay..." and so on.

God always hears that one...and always answers.

Then we make some faith-based decisions to apprehend our newly minted destiny and find ourselves nowhere near what the promise sounded like.

Sort of like... Behold, this is Leah!

God's played Laban on you.

And we go to Him and say, "What's this that you have done to me?" He responds like Laban.

"Giving the younger before the firstborn is not so done in our country." Or in other words, "It's not done so in the Kingdom to give a promise ahead of a process."

Laban then tells Jacob to finish Leah's wedding week. Then he would give him Rachel. That means honour Leah, make love to her, and give her a honeymoon; then I will give you Rachel. God says, "Honour your process, be fruitful in your process, finish your process, and I will prepare and lead you into your promise."

LOVED AND UNFRUITFUL, UNLOVED AND FRUITFUL

The next part is interesting.

Genesis 29:31
*When the Lord saw that **Leah was hated, he opened her womb, but Rachel was barren.***

God saw that Jacob didn't love Leah but hated her. So, he made her fruitful, but he left Rachel barren.

As long as you resist processes in your life, your promises will remain barren. God isn't doing that to punish you. But if you don't gain the preparation the process provides, your promise will destroy you. He won't release a promise that will destroy you because He loves you.

My son loves driving. The independence, I think, is what always has attracted him to want to drive. He would ask and ask to drive the car.

I think of myself as a loving father. I'm happy to give stuff to my kids. I could've just said yes and invited him to drive until his heart's content. The problem was that he was asking when he was six. Giving him the freedom to drive at that age would've been abusive, not loving. It would have set him up for accidents, perhaps even death!

In the same way, God knows what He wants to give, and He can also tell if we are ready.

As an aside, generally, deserts get us limping to the point that we never really feel ready. That's when He says, "Great, now you're ready."

Want to know why?

> *Song of Solomon 8:5a*
> *Who is that coming up from the wilderness, **leaning on her beloved**?*

SONS IN THE DESERT

So Rachel, the promise, is left barren, but Leah bears some sons. Reuben, Simeon, Levi, and Judah.

REUBEN

Reuben means to behold or to see.

> *Genesis 29:32*
> *"Because the **Lord** has looked upon my affliction."*

In your process, you learn how to see. Things are going slow enough that you learn how to see a vision and how to see people. You learn how to see obstacles and opportunities. You learn how to see what's hidden and what's in plain sight.

You learn how to see gifts in people. You learn how to see the Holy Spirit moving.

You learn how to see.

If you were to drive a little minivan at 50 KM (30MPH), you need to know how to see. But if you are driving a Ferrari at 200KM (125MPH), you need to see...better.

Similarly, in your process, you learn how to see because, in your promise, you need to know how to see because you're moving faster, the stakes are higher, and the road is sometimes treacherous.

With Leah, your desert, your process, you get Reuben.

SIMEON

Then she bears her second son Simeon.

Genesis 29:33
> *"Because the Lord has heard that I am hated, he has given me this son also."*

Simeon means to hear.

In your process, you learn how to hear. How to hear people, how to hear God, how to hear the rustling of the Holy Spirit. How to hear the truth, how to hear wounds behind words. How to hear God in the moment, not just in the quiet place.

You learn how to hear.

When you're with Rachel, you don't have time to learn how to hear; you need to know how to hear. You're going too fast with Rachel; there are more voices because it generally isn't as quiet with Rachel as with Leah. So, you have to be able to recognize His voice amongst the many.

With Leah, in your desert, in your process, you get Simeon.

LEVI

Then Leah had Levi.

> *Genesis 29:34*
> *"Now, this time, my husband will be attached to me because I have borne him three sons."*

Levi means joined to attached.

You learn intimacy with God when you're with Leah. So many times, I find myself in conversations with young leaders whose anointing or ministry is their identity. I find myself speaking with people who again identify themselves in what they do rather than who they are in Jesus.

It is a dangerous game to have who I am depending upon what I do. It's religion's trap.

This is where we get our limp. Because when we are with Leah, we frankly don't want anyone to know. It's embarrassing to be doing something less important when you've declared that God has something great for you to do.

Rachel is big. She is the promise that can lead to influence, fame, and importance. Selfishness, pride, and arrogance can lurk in the murky waters of success. If our hearts aren't genuinely attached to Jesus, we can lose our way fairly quickly, and the promise's success can override the promise's purpose very quickly.

It is with Leah, in your desert, in your process, that you get Levi.

JUDAH

Then she bears another son, Judah.

Genesis 29:35
"This time, I will praise the Lord."

Judah means praise.

In your desert or process, you learn the power of worship. You learn how worship creates a connection with God and sets the atmosphere in any situation. You learn how worship and praise become a source of strength, intimacy, and clarity. You learn to become a worshiper, not just one who worships at events.

You learn the oasis of His presence when you have become so weak and thirsty that you can only close your eyes and reach out and just say, "Abba."

> *It's with Leah where the heart of the lover is born so it can give birth to a king.*

It's with Leah where the heart of the lover is born so it can give birth to a king.

Skill for spiritual warfare, intimacy, leadership, and revelation happen in these dry seasons of process. When you are with Rachel, these attributes need to be established to make us into Spirit-led stewards of the promise.

It is with Leah, in your desert, in your process, that you get Judah.

How do you know you're in a desert and not a storm?

You chose to take the invitation of the Lord.

How do you know you're with Leah?

What was promised and what you possess are two different things.

What do you do with that?

Honour Leah's week, and she will bear sons for you.

You Can Love Her

My desert was attached to my call to ministry. I received the call to ministry when I was fourteen and went to Bible college for a year after graduating high school to answer that call. But I got disillusioned during college and decided, while not running from my faith, I would run from the call.

Cathy and I met in Bible college and married shortly after. In those years, work and purpose were hard to find, and I worked in construction as a commercial/industrial insulator. Not a fun job; it paid the bills, my boss was a deacon member at our church, my coworkers all loved Jesus, and it was stable. But I was miserable.

Everything that I tried to establish from a career standpoint fell through. Teaching, policing, broadcasting, and many other "ideas" never panned out. After insulating for four years, I came to the point where I knew that I was running from my call and submitted to the call. But in truth, not because I wanted to follow Jesus as a minister but to get out of insulating.

That attitude would result in a lengthy multi-year process to prepare me for the promise, but I didn't realize that then. I had my moment at the altar; I had prayed the dangerous prayer I shared earlier and was ready to step into my destiny!

Shortly after I decided to answer the call, a church approached me with an offer as a worship and youth pastor. I immediately said yes, and to give you a sense of my attitude, I wasn't surprised they wanted me. I was young, talented, could communicate, and would likely be a fantastic choice.

After two months of talking, planning, and me dreaming, the church rescinded its offer and chose someone else.

I was devastated. And no one else showed interest for the next year until the same church called again.

They had a church split, were rebuilding, and needed a worship and youth pastor. The same pastor asked me to join his team again.

I said yes, no prayer needed! Anything to get out of insulating. Their financial offer would have amounted to about one-quarter of what we would have needed, but I was ready to go anyway.

After two months of talking, planning, me dreaming, and my wife worrying about how we would ever do this, the church rescinded their offer.

I was devastated again, fell into a depression, and lost hope about going into ministry. I questioned whether I had heard from God and frankly began to fail in my faith.

I was a lousy employee, husband, young father, and Christ follower.

About eight months into my malaise, I was working with one of my friends on our insulating crew on a large duct. We were on a scaffold about twenty-five feet high passing material to one another as we insulated a duct about six feet in diameter.

As we were working, my friend said, "Landen, I had a dream last night about you, and God asked me to ask you a question." I replied that God hadn't spoken to me much, so if he'd heard something, I guessed I'd be willing to listen.

My friend said, "God asked me to ask you if you have been found faithful with what He has given you?" The conviction of the Spirit hit me so hard that I slumped to my knees and began to weep. Not polite little crying, but the ugly kind of heaving sobs. All the pain and frustration of the desert season burst through. My friend crawled under the duct, knelt beside me, and wept with me, and I repented for my unfaithfulness to the process.

I returned home a changed man. I fell back in love with Jesus, began loving my wife like a godly man should, poured myself into my local church, and poured myself back into my job.

And I fell in love with the process; with Leah.

We forged a city-wide children's ministry and tapped into my apostolic leanings before I understood what they were. I leaned into our worship ministry and became our worship pastor's number two, serving him and the church in regular worship leading. I learned ministry, servant-hood, humility, faith, and joy. I learned to see, to hear, to be at one with, and to worship.

After a year, the same church called that had twice broken my heart.

BE FOUND BY SERVING

The call came while I was in my worship pastor's office. I was at the church in the evening and noticed he hadn't had time to put away the sheet music from the last five or six Sundays. So, I went in and began to file the music away.

> *Destiny will never be found by searching, but it will be found by serving.*

I share this because it is an essential part of the story. I was found serving. Destiny will never be found by searching, but it will be found by serving. Or maybe even said a better way, destiny will find you if you're serving.

David's destiny was unlocked when he killed Goliath. Why was he there? He was serving his dad by bringing food to the front. Moses was serving his father-in-law Jethro when he met God at the burning bush. Joseph was serving the jailer when he was called to serve Pharoah. Samuel was serving Eli when he heard the voice of God. Nehemiah was serving Artaxerxes when he was called to rebuild the walls of Jerusalem. I could go on, Ruth and Naomi, Elisha and Elijah, Paul, and Timothy, even Jesus, served His earthly father before He entered the ministry.

Look through the Bible and see how serving unlocked destiny.

A new pastor had taken over and had heard of me. "Your name continues to come up in our discussion, I don't know you, but I feel that you are supposed to be here. Would you consider joining my team?" My first responses to the other two invitations were "yes" immediately, but now I was in love with where I was; I had experienced Leah's faithfulness to me because she gave me Reuben, Simeon, Levi, and Judah. I wasn't sure I wanted to leave and replied that I needed to pray.

I think Jacob loved Leah. Genesis 49 proves it for me.

Genesis 49:31-33

*There they buried Abraham and Sarah his wife. There they buried Isaac and Rebekah his wife, **and there I buried Leah**—the field and the cave that is in it were bought from the Hittites." When Jacob finished commanding his sons, he drew up his feet into the bed and breathed his last, and was gathered to his people.*

Jacob asked to be buried beside Leah, and if you truly embrace your processes, you will look back upon them, see the fruit they bore, and be forever grateful.

We prayed, felt the call to follow Jesus, and at the time of this writing, started our journey in ministry over 27 years ago; and Jesus remains faithful to us and we have tried to be faithful to Him.

How Long?

There will be deserts in every Christ follower's life.

For some, they may be shorter than for others. You might go through a lengthy wilderness when answers seem few and far between.

Regardless of whether you are in a storm or desert, faithfulness brings fruitfulness. This means you can bear great fruit even during your desert or storm.

For example, I would like to share the story of a man I knew named Willie. Willie was a postman, not grand or important, just very ordinary. He loved making wooden toys. Willie made charming doll houses, trucks, and tractors for kids. He loved animals. He would take in every stray, loved his little hobby farm, and most of all, his wife, Annette, and their daughter, Abigail.

Willie passed away recently from pancreatic cancer. Yet he was a miracle. You might ask how that could be because he's gone now. That is understandable. Indeed, his diagnosis was dire and given to him seven years prior, but it was a diagnosis that said that he would only live six months. Yet he ended up having seven years.

Seven years of never saying he had cancer but was fighting one. He would never complain but instead pressed in the clutch of faithfulness and continued to bear more and more fruit.

I tear up when I think of sitting with him on his deathbed, praying for a miracle. Once, he quietly reminded me that he had been living one for the past several years.

What an amazing man. Quiet, humble, simple. Not great by our standards. Not a mighty looking oak, but fruitful. So fruitful.

Hundreds and hundreds of people gathered to honour Willie. Because he was a man worth honouring, he was worth mourning. He was fruitful. And even in the storm, he slept and let Jesus navigate.

In Mark 11, we read where Jesus curses a fig tree and learn an essential lesson for sustaining grace.

> *Mark 11:12-14*
> *On the following day, when they came from Bethany, He was hungry. And seeing in the distance **a fig tree in leaf**, He went to see if He could find anything on it. When He came to it, **He found nothing but leaves, for it was not the season for figs**. And He said to it, "May no one ever eat fruit from you again." And His disciples heard it.*

There is a profound lesson in this passage. The tree was leafy, but Jesus couldn't find any fruit. However, it wasn't the tree's fault; it wasn't the season for figs. It doesn't seem fair that Jesus would curse the tree if it weren't the regular fruit-bearing season.

This brings us face to face with an important lesson attached to moving forward in this gear of grace.

Jesus has the prerogative to expect fruit from our lives even when the "season" we're in would suggest it is impossible.

He will expect fruitfulness from us in our desert seasons, in our processes, in our pain, and our perplexity. Why? Because, in the desert, the pain, and the confusion, we come to the end of ourselves and discover the power of being filled with the Spirit. It's like the process chokes out any sense of our strength to sustain us, and we have nothing left but the Spirit to empower us.

You can't escape Jacob's limp if you want to walk at destiny speed, and the crucible of the desert will break the mindset of being able to do it in our own strength versus the power of the Spirit. As painful as those seasons can be, regardless of their duration, God's sustaining grace empowers us to bear fruit when it would seem like there is no hope.

Willie knew what sustaining grace was. He bore fruit when no fruit should've been borne.

Tangie shared earlier about her husband's journey through liver disease. Those two are heroes to me. I have never seen people bear so much fruit in dry and stormy places. Yes, there were tears and there were doubts. But there was sustaining grace; they remained faithful and they were found fruitful.

We can't force the end of the desert, but we can shift into the next gear regardless of our circumstances because even in brokenness, we can still move at destiny speed and into our final gear.

Clutch Prayer – Repent

Lord Jesus, thank You for Your love, grace, and power. I thank You that You are with me. You promised never to leave me or forsake me. This is a painful season; I'm tired and need You. I repent for resisting the process and trying to protect myself. I ask You to forgive me for where I have been fighting against Your purposes in the process. I invite You to sustain me through the wilderness. I choose to worship instead of worry and faith instead of fear.

I love You and need You more than ever.

I pray for the strength to trust you more.

In Jesus' name,

Amen

A Quick Review

The fifth Gear of Grace is Sustaining Grace—grace to wander the wilderness.

The tension is to turn and go back to Egypt!

The clutch is faithfulness.

The clutch of faithfulness is faithfulness that brings fruitfulness regardless of the circumstance.

Study Questions

If you are in a group study, share some testimonies of when you have walked in Sustaining Grace.

What areas has God been challenging you in during your process?

How can you guard yourself against not bearing fruit in this season?

Where can you serve to be found?

Renew - How is the Holy Spirit challenging your trust levels with God through your process? (Remember you can bear fruit in and out of season)

Respond - How will you respond to the question, "Has God found you faithful with what He has given you?"

CHAPTER 9

SIXTH GEAR: RADICAL OBEDIENCE

LIVES OF IMPACT

John 14:11-14

*Believe Me that I am in the Father and the Father is in Me or else **believe on account of the works themselves**. "Truly, truly, I say to you, whoever believes in Me **will also do the works that I do; and greater works than these will he do**, because I am going to the Father. **Whatever you ask in My Name, this I will do**, that the Father may be glorified in the Son. If you **ask Me anything in My Name, I will do it.***

John 3:34

*For He whom God has sent utters the words of God, for **He gives the Spirit without measure.***

THE SIXTH AND FINAL GEAR OF GRACE WE WILL EXPLORE IS radical obedience.

At the start of this Chapter, I want to address what I feel the enemy would use as a lie to rob every believer from shifting into this gear.

An Early Mistake

When I first began to explore the Gears of Grace, I mistakenly shared that this sixth gear, Radical Obedience, was not necessarily a gear all people would engage in. I initially thought this gear was for the heroes of our past and present. Great leaders like Smith Wigglesworth, John G Lake, or Kathryn Kuhlman. Or those in our present day like Billy Graham, Heidi Baker, Bill Johnson, Randy Clark, and the like. People who have seen and are seeing thousands impacted by their ministries.

And there, indeed, are few like those I just listed, who live in this gear, but all of us are permitted to shift into this gear.

A subtle lie sown by the enemy into the hearts of regular Christians is that impact is reserved for those who appear to be great in the Kingdom. This lie robs many of us of destiny speed simply because we don't believe we are entitled to destiny.

Think of it this way.

The Kingdom

Let's look at the Kingdom of God using a medieval king and kingdom as our example, where there are different classes of society— the nobility, who have wealth and the favour of the king. There would be mighty knights and warriors who have a relationship with the king based upon their shared battles and victories. Then there are the lower classes, from shopkeepers to small business owners, down to peasants and slaves.

Each class down seems to find itself further and further from actual contact with the king.

Whether consciously or unconsciously, we look at the lives or ministries of other people who have somehow, like the nobility, through birth or just unmerited favour, or like the knighthood, with their acts of selfless valour, as being given special status for access to the king.

THE LEVELLING CROSS

I am sharing this with you because most will read about these fourth, fifth, and sixth gears through the lens of assuming there are classes in the Kingdom and will just adopt a belief that favour with God to have a life like this, just "isn't for the likes of me/us."

And like the farmer who tells his son that knighthood isn't for him because of his class, or the servant girl told not to dream of being an artist because she will always be a servant, the enemy tries to hold people to the class of their birth.

He asks, "Who are you to think that you can have more?"

He further taunts and accuses, "You can never have more; you can't enjoy the King's favour because you have been born into the low class. You have been born into insignificance, and to aspire to anything other than insignificance is self-promoting, prideful arrogance."

There is a wonderfully liberating answer to all those accusations.

I have been *born again*.

The class system takes away choice. I enjoy stories where the unlikely hero, born outside the favoured classes, rises to greatness. The plucky servant girl or determined stable boy both refuse to believe their birth should determine their greatness. We all enjoy the stories of those who rise above the obstacles of their class and the resistance of naysayers around them who resent their determination. We connect to their fight against cynics whose jealousy fuels their awful words and attempts to ruin the determination of our heroes, while secretly wishing they could be great as well.

However, the Cross is the great leveller of the classes. Jesus' expression of love to humanity through the Cross removed the forcible confinement of class by birth giving us the freedom to choose Him and be born again.

Galatians 3:26-29

For in Christ Jesus you are all sons of God, through faith. For as many of you as were baptized into Christ have put on Christ. There is neither Jew nor Greek, there is neither slave nor free, there is no male and female, for you are all one in Christ Jesus. And if you are Christ's, then you are Abraham's offspring, heirs according to promise.

Paul picks three unique examples of class division—Jew or Greek, male or female, and slave or free. Three mindsets are attached to these examples.

JEW OR GREEK

The first mindset is entitlement. The Jews considered themselves entitled to a relationship with God that Greeks or Gentiles would never have on account of the Abrahamic covenant and the Law. A mindset of entitlement leads to the deception of superiority. Paul points out that Jesus had dissolved any thought of a higher class of nobles in the Kingdom through the Cross. The religious spirit flourishes in the atmosphere of superiority. The Cross removed every possible division created within humanity, and affirmed each individual's value based on His love for them not their righteous performance. Grace is our entry into His Kingdom, so no one can assume greater value than anyone else.

Ephesians 2:8-9

**For by grace you have been saved through faith. And
this is not your own doing; it is the gift of God, *not a
result of works*, so that no one may boast.**

At an intellectual level, I think most of us understand this
Scripture. However, in the day-to-day living out of our faith, we tend
to consistently get duped into returning to the mindset of entitlement
by earning our favour with God through religious activity.

The thing about grace is that it requires us to humble ourselves.
How we usually personally deal with sin is to put ourselves on a
"spiritual time out" and distance ourselves from the Lord after falling
short. And we think the distance punishes us and allows us to earn our
way back into His presence.

Romans 11:6

**But if it is by grace, it is *no longer based on works;*
otherwise *grace would no longer be grace.***

The humility required to receive God's favour confidently and to
come before his throne of grace (Heb. 4:16) is counter-intuitive. Yet
we can begin to enjoy His goodness when we humble ourselves and
recognize that we are without any recourse other than His grace.

SLAVE OR FREE

The second mindset is lack of value. A slave was a piece of property,
used and abused at the whim of the master. Slavery was a huge industry
in Paul's day and it constituted for a very interesting dynamic in his
church plants where slaves and freeborn people worshiped side by side,
discovering they were equals in value to Jesus. A mentality of lack of
value leads to unworthiness, and unworthiness robs people of love.

Luke 12:6-7

Are not five sparrows sold for two pennies? And not one of them is forgotten before God. Why, even the hairs of your head are all numbered. Fear not; you are of more value than many sparrows.

There is an epidemic of believers who have embraced unworthiness and have robbed themselves of the wonder of destiny speed and, with it, are deprived of experiencing the love of God. Not the love we know He ultimately has for all humanity, but the doting love of a fully engaged Father.

To the unworthy soul, the thought of being doted upon sounds like a fairy tale, like a slave's dream of freedom.

Sweet Jesus again destroys the lack of value on the Cross. By dying once and for all, He proved that each person holds infinite value to God. He didn't just die for some; He died for all.

The trouble with grace is that it requires us to accept how much God values us.

Mark 10:45

"For even the Son of Man came not to be served but to serve, and to give His life as a ransom for many."

The trouble with grace is that it requires us to accept how much God values us. The thought that He would ransom us forces us to reconsider our value. Grace calls us to live up to our worth and reject the mindset of a trapped slave, and live free.

MALE OR FEMALE

The third mindset is selective authority. In Paul's day, women didn't have authority and were treated like property. The thought of a woman having any authority would seem ridiculous to the established society of the time.

In the same way, many of us have bought into the mindset that God gives authority to some but not others. This mindset leads to apathy, where we begin to think that we can't do it, so hopefully, someone with more authority will.

Philippians 4:13
I can do all things through Him who strengthens me.

Grace, however, empowers us to believe by faith. Faith isn't the feeling of belief; it is the assurance of fact and not founded in outcomes. But, as I shared in the gear of authority, its foundation is in the resurrection of Jesus.

Remember, if you are convinced in the gospel of the good news of the resurrection, you possess the faith necessary to move mountains. Instead of faith based on the feeling of belief, we base it on the fact of Jesus' resurrection.

On the Cross, Jesus levelled the playing field once more, giving authority to all who believe in Him.

If you have been trapped in any of these three mindsets, pray the prayer of repentance below, and let's move forward into this exciting gear of radical obedience.

Wonderful Jesus, Your Cross made us all equal in our potential. I realize now that these mindsets have robbed me of fully engaging in faith-filled obedience. I repent for those strongholds of thought and choose to engage the truth. I invite you Holy Spirit to convict me when I am tempted to return to those old mindsets and to fill me with the strength to follow Your lead with confidence and Joy.

In Jesus' Name,

Amen

So, all of us who have chosen to follow and believe in Jesus are qualified to walk in radical obedience. However, and this is important, radical obedience doesn't look the same for every person. Some are meant to live in that gear; others are intended to shift into it occasionally.

Neither person holds more value to God, and He will reward both disciples for acting in obedience, simply doing what He has asked us to do.

THE TENSION – THE SIZE OF THE TASK

The tasks God asks of us can grow to an immense size requiring the disciple to face real tension.

Mark 10:27
Jesus looked at them and said, "With man it is impossible, but not with God. For all things are possible with God.

Again, this sixth gear, Radical Obedience, is for everyone. Some may end up living there, and others will shift into radical obedience as God leads.

This Kingdom isn't about comparison but obedience. God will ask some to live in this gear, consistently leaning into the "all things are possible" God, as a life assignment or call. All of us, however, are meant to shift into radical obedience on occasion. A telltale sign of a disciple maturing and experiencing a life of destiny is that they occasionally shift into this sixth gear.

To one like Heidi Baker, feeding a nation would be the impossible call to a life of radical obedience God gave her. To a steelworker who loves Jesus, giving a car away might be the tension he faces in radical obedience, and to a widow in Africa, the tension of radical obedience may be giving away her last penny to a blind beggar.

Every act of obedience receives the positive attention of heaven.

What radical obedience looks like varies from individual to individual; the point is not to compare one to another. The value of obedience isn't determined by its size, and there is no such thing as insignificant obedience. Every act of obedience receives the positive attention of heaven.

Matthew 10:42
*"And whoever gives one of these little ones **even a cup of cold water** because he is a disciple, truly, I say to you, he **will by no means lose his reward**."*

However, many of us don't know how to manage the tension and try to avoid it because we don't know how to disarm it.

THE CLUTCH – FAITH THAT LOOKS

You might think, "But the Bible says, walk by faith, not sight. So how are we supposed to have faith that looks?"

Matthew 17:20
*He said to them, "Because of **your little faith**. For truly, I say to you, if you have **faith like a grain of mustard seed**, you will say to this mountain, 'Move from here to there,' and it will move, and **nothing will be impossible for you**."*

As I shared earlier in the book, great faith isn't rooted in an outcome but in Jesus' resurrection. As a reminder, if you believe Jesus rose from the dead, you possess the faith necessary to move mountains. But at the same time, there's a real tension we feel that's ultimately rooted in fear leading us to worry about outcomes when we step into radical obedience.

Worry is very real. It is also very demonic. I have often fallen prey to worry because it feels like I'm being responsible. When we are afraid, we feel like we must do something, much like the fight-or-flight response. Worry takes effort, and because of the effort and energy spent on it, it can become empowered to deceive to us into feeling like we've done something about the issue we're facing.

The problem is worry accomplishes nothing. It just saps our strength and energy without changing or affecting our circumstances at all.

Philippians 4:4-7

*Rejoice in the Lord always; again I will say, rejoice. Let your reasonableness be known to everyone. The Lord is at hand; **do not be anxious about anything**, but in everything by **prayer and supplication with thanksgiving let your requests be made known to God.** And **the peace of God, which surpasses all understanding, will guard your hearts and your minds in Christ Jesus.***

We're supposed to be able to live in peace as Christians. We're supposed to live in an otherworldly peace which frankly doesn't make sense. In Philippians, Paul refers to it as a peace that surpasses our understanding. We're supposed to face circumstances at total rest without any worry. But often, we don't. We don't because we can be deceived into thinking that breakthrough gives us peace, in the hope that the outer circumstances of our lives will result in peace for our inner man.

When we perceive the peace of God from this perspective, we open ourselves to confusion. Our peace, the peace of God, isn't subject to circumstance; its experience is made available in our inner man regardless of what may be happening circumstantially.

> *Ephesians 3:16-21*
> *That according to the riches of His glory, He may grant you to be strengthened with power through his Spirit in your inner being, so that Christ may dwell in your hearts through faith—that you, being rooted and grounded in love, may have strength to comprehend with all the saints what is the breadth and length and height and depth, and to know the love of Christ that surpasses knowledge, that you may be filled with all the fullness of God.*
>
> *Now to Him who is able to do far more abundantly than all that we ask or think, according to the power at work within us, to Him be glory in the church and in Christ Jesus throughout all generations, forever and ever. Amen.*

Faith is a commitment to conviction. A conviction is born in the inner man, not through circumstances.

COMBATING WORRY – THE POWER OF THE TRADE

Worry and concern are two different things. Worry is a response, and concern is a gateway to a response.

> *1 Peter 5:7 (AMPC)*
> *Casting the whole of your care [all your anxieties, all your worries, all your concerns, once and for all] on Him, for He cares for you affectionately and cares about you watchfully.*

There are going to be things that we face that will cause concern. Whether it is a financial crisis, relational tension, or a bad medical report, all of us, at one time or another, will find ourselves facing a concern.

However, what we do with that concern will determine whether we will find peace or inner turmoil. As I have said before, the peace of God is not subject to circumstances, but to access that peace, we need to know how to manage our concerns.

So, when faced with a concern, we need to look at it like it's a gateway to a response, like an opportunity to reveal our faith.

Ultimately worry is hell's form of faith. True faith will agree with God's promises. Worry chooses to agree with hell's threats.

When we're at the gateway of concern, we have two choices. Worry, the faith of hell leading to anxiety, or entering into the rest of heaven by faith.

So how do we do it? Is it possible to address our concerns while simultaneously bringing strength to our inner man promised in Ephesians?

Yes! Yes! Yes! By making a trade and being irresponsible.

Matthew 11:28-30

*Come to Me, **all who labour and are heavy laden**, and I will give you rest. Take My yoke upon you, and learn from Me, for I am gentle and lowly in heart, and you will find rest for your souls. For My yoke is easy, and My burden is light."*

The way that we can do this is by trading our worry for waiting on the Lord. Look at the Scriptures below.

Isaiah 40:31

**But they who wait for the Lord shall renew their
    strength;**
they shall mount up with wings like eagles;
they shall run and not be weary;
they shall walk and not faint.

Proverbs 8:34-35

Blessed is the one who listens to Me,
watching daily at My gates,
waiting beside My doors.
For whoever finds Me finds life
and obtains favour from the Lord.

The Bible promises that the glory of the Lord would be our rear guard (Isa. 58:8). The word for "glory" in the original language is "*kabod*" which means weight. Waiting on the Lord strengthens our inner man to manage the revelatory weight of what God wants to reveal to us. Many people desire the weighty things of God but are unwilling to develop the inner strength to bear the weight and, as a result, miss out on the glory of God being their rear guard.

What does waiting look like? Well, waiting starts by looking like... waiting. Shutting down your phone, turning off the television, logging off, and turning on some worship music and start to just rest in Him.

Waiting matures as it becomes a natural posture.

Psalms 123:2

Behold, as the eyes of servants
look to the hand of their master,
as the eyes of a maidservant
to the hand of her mistress,
so our eyes look to the Lord our God,
till He has mercy upon us.

We can live in rest by simply waiting on God and looking toward Him continually. It's living life with the eyes of our hearts focused on the Lord throughout our day and choosing to be determined to live in an open conversation with Him.

Worry feels responsible, and rest feels irresponsible. But when we trade our worry for waiting, we posture ourselves to experience the rest Jesus promised as we trade yokes with Him. The truth is rest is the most responsible thing you can do with your concerns. Because in the rest, God will reveal the proper response so that when you act, you act in the wisdom of Heaven. This revelatory response to our concerns sets us up for victory.

THE ROLE OF THE SPIRIT

Ephesians 1:17-21

*That the God of our Lord Jesus Christ, the Father of glory, **may give you the Spirit of wisdom and of revelation** in the knowledge of Him, **having the eyes of your hearts enlightened,** that you may **know what is the hope to which He has called you,** what are the **riches of His glorious inheritance in the saints,** and what is **the immeasurable greatness of His power toward us who believe,** according to the **working of His great might that He worked in Christ when He raised Him from the dead** and seated Him at his right hand in the Heavenly places, **far above all rule and authority and power and dominion, and above every name that is named, not only in this age but also in the one to come.***

Amid radical obedience, the Holy Spirit is revealed as our source of wisdom and revelation. Wisdom and revelation are necessary in radical obedience because we would be left open to the enemy's retaliation without them.

Satan's attack on believers is very real. Whether through persecution, lies, sickness or disease, or discouragement, the enemy's attack can be devastating. However, I see a possible route of obedience in Scripture that leaves the enemy without response to a disciple's choice to obey God radically.

THE NECESSITY OF REVELATION

In both the fourth gear of empowerment and especially in this sixth gear of radical obedience, the ability to manage revelatory thought is necessary.

Revelation is simply when the Holy Spirit awakens our conscious understanding of an element of the nature of God that we hadn't understood before. Let me give an example of revelation from my own life.

I spent many years in ministry, not fully understanding the goodness of God. My doctrine had led me to believe that God was good but would bring sickness, disease, or dire circumstances to us to teach us or call us back into holiness or relationship. At the same time, our decisions can lead us down the road to challenges like those listed above, and He can use those things to bring us back or deepen our faith.

Then I was exposed to some teaching about the goodness of God and that He wasn't responsible for sickness and dire circumstances. As I began to search the Word, it became clear that I was limited in my faith because of faulty doctrine in this area. Once I renovated my thinking on the goodness of God, I began to see miracles happen at a far greater level. That revelatory thought transformed my life and ministry. It changed my view of God as a good Father and unlocked new realms of intimacy with Him that I had never known before.

Gone are the fears of His retribution for when I have fallen short, and I now know the love of a good Father.

LET'S NOT BE AFRAID

The spirit of religion depends on fear. And new revelation is an area where the established religious spirits will attack with fear. But we needn't be afraid; there are some important ways to manage revelation, so we don't get off track. Read the following Scripture, and we will discuss some powerful elements of revelation. The first four elements of this will be foundational, but the last element will be liberating and perhaps fun.

> *Ephesians 3:2-6*
>
> *...assuming that you have heard of the **stewardship of God's grace** that was given to me for you, how **the mystery was made known to me by revelation,** as I have written briefly. When you read this, you can **perceive my insight into the mystery of Christ,** which was **not made known to the sons of men in other generations** as it has now been **revealed** to His holy apostles and prophets **by the Spirit.** This mystery is that the Gentiles are fellow heirs, members of the same body, and partakers of the promise in Christ Jesus through the Gospel.*

REVELATION IS NOT EXTRA-BIBLICAL – *PERCEIVE MY INSIGHT INTO THE MYSTERY OF CHRIST*

Paul shared with the Ephesians that he had received a mystery. A revelation. Now, this is important to understand about revelation; it is not extra-biblical. It is not something outside of God's nature or character; instead, it is the uncovering of His nature, and His Word confirms it.

Here Paul receives a revelation from the Lord about the Gentiles. The Spirit reveals to him that they should also receive the gospel. The Law would no longer be the bridge of connection with God. He wanted a relationship with all men, not just the Jews. Paul was an expert in scripture and as a result of the Gospel lifting off his former Pharisaical lens of interpretation, he could see what God had said centuries earlier about His heart for the world. The following scripture in Isaiah would be one of those scriptures Paul would have been so familiar with but needed the Holy Spirit to reveal what it truly meant. I love how the Message version rendered this verse and I've highlighted in bold the revelation.

Isaiah 49:6 (MSG)
*He says, "But that's **not a big enough job for my Servant—***
just to recover the tribes of Jacob,
merely to round up the strays of Israel.
I'm setting you up as a light for the nations
so that my salvation becomes global!"

Paul would have seen the greater narrative of Scripture pointing to this revelation about the Gentiles. How did that revelation happen? Paul doesn't say, but I've experienced revelation in three ways.

The first way is through the reading of the Word of God. Revelation from the Word doesn't happen through the mechanical religious reading of the Bible. But as I have pondered a thought or asked the Holy Spirit to read with me and enlighten my heart as I read, suddenly something will jump out from the Scriptures awakening me to something that would seem new about the nature of God. Still, He had said it about Himself long ago, but I'm just seeing it now.

The second way is through teaching. Often while I sit under the anointed teaching of the Word of God, something awakens my heart to fresh revelation, or the Holy Spirit uses something taught to launch me into a different train of revelatory thought.

The third way is through waiting on the Lord in worship. Most of the time, this is where I receive the majority of revelations. In the quiet place, while waiting on the Lord, He drops something into my heart that awakens my conscious understanding of His goodness. From there, I search Scripture to confirm what the Holy Spirit has spoken to me.

An important principle comes into play when you wait on the Lord and hear from Him. Our integrity requires that we don't search scripture *to prove* but rather *for proof.* We don't want to allow ourselves to twist the Word to make it fit into what we feel the Holy Spirit has said but instead invite the Lord to show us where He's already said what we are discovering.

CHALLENGES OUR PRESENT UNDERSTANDING – *THE MYSTERY IS THAT THE GENTILES ARE FELLOW HEIRS*

Paul must have been shocked, confused, and even outraged when he read through a passage like the one I quoted in Isaiah. Were the Gentiles meant to receive salvation? It must have been shocking to look at the Scriptures with new insight to see that God had been saying this all along.

Why make it hard to understand? Why not just make it plain?

When God speaks *beyond* our understanding, He is doing it to protect His Word from being corrupted *by* our understanding. Furthermore, the point of revelation, the point of mystery, is to change our understanding, not yield to it.

It's not about my understanding; it's about me coming to an understanding.

Your change is the desired outcome of revelation; it is intended to bring you into more profound connection, authority, anointing, and expressions of Him to you and the world through you. However, when our understanding is offended by what God reveals, should we choose to dismiss it, we'll miss out on the power available to us had we walked in the activation of the new understanding.

PERFECTLY TIMED – *NOT MADE KNOWN TO THE SONS OF MEN IN OTHER GENERATIONS*

I often hear people lament about different revelations they have recently received, saying that they wished they had known these new truths years earlier.

The enemy will do anything to make us feel like we don't measure up. He will accuse us of not being good enough, even as God reveals Himself in a new and exciting way. This is a demonic attack, continually leaving us feeling like we still are unworthy even though God is dynamically speaking to us in that very moment.

The fact is, God reveals Himself to us at perfectly timed moments, so there is a convergence with our maturity, wisdom, position, location, and relationships to maximize the impact of the revelation.

An even deeper truth is when we question the timing of God revealing Himself to us, we question His wisdom.

God will reveal new elements of His nature to you in perfectly timed moments. The more significant issue is what we do with what He shares.

REVELATION MUST BE STEWARDED – *THE STEWARDSHIP OF GOD'S GRACE GIVEN TO ME FOR YOU*

Jesus warned us to pay attention to what we hear.

Mark 4:24-25 (ESV)

And He said to them, "Pay attention to what you hear: with the measure you use, it will be measured to you, and still more will be added to you. For to the one who has, more will be given, and from the one who has not, even what he has will be taken away."

There has not been a time in the church's history when more information and revelation is available to the Body of Christ. There is such an abundance of rich teaching and writing in this day and age that there is no excuse for any disciple to live in spiritual ignorance.

Unfortunately, the spirit of consumerism has managed to weasel its way even into the beautiful bounty of wisdom available to the church. As such, we have become more interested in acquiring knowledge than actually applying it. To the consumer, acquisition holds more significant value than application. Just take a moment to let that sink in.

Revelation simply acquired is fattening; revelation applied is power.

We have a responsibility as believers in Jesus to apply what is revealed to us in the timing it is given because there is great purpose in responding when we are given fresh revelation into a matter. This is where it can get fun.

REVELATION: RELIGION'S GREATEST FEAR – SATAN'S LOST PRIVILEGE

Please take your time through this next section and meditate on it because it is so exciting!

Hell fears revelation because revelation sends it into confusion. When God reveals a new element of His nature, hell is left reeling.

Take a look at this scripture.

> *Ephesians 3:8-10*
> *To me, though I am the very least of all the saints, this grace was given, to preach to the Gentiles the unsearchable riches of Christ, and to bring to light for everyone what is the plan of the mystery hidden for ages in God who created all things, **so that through the church the manifold wisdom of God might now be made known to the rulers and authorities in the heavenly places.***

One of the biggest lies that hell throws our way is that Satan knows more about God than we do.

Not true.

Right now, in Heaven, God is revealing Himself to the Heavenly Hosts.

> *Revelation 4:8-11*
> *And the four living creatures, each of them with six wings, **are full of eyes all around and within, and day and night they never cease to say,** "Holy, holy, holy, is the Lord God Almighty, who was and is and is to come!"*

And whenever the living creatures give glory and
honour and thanks to Him who is seated on the throne,
who lives forever and ever, the twenty-four elders fall
down before Him who is seated on the throne and
worship Him who lives forever and ever. They cast
their crowns before the throne, saying,

"Worthy are you, our Lord and God,
to receive glory and honour and power,
for you created all things,
and by your will they existed and were created."

At first glance, this seems to be a pretty boring life. Are they just saying holy, holy, holy, all the time? Why would they do that?

Those creatures, full of eyes, are uniquely created to see something new about God every time they look at Him. That new revelation of His goodness makes them cry, "Holy, holy, holy." Those creatures and the elders live in the perpetual revelation of the nature of our infinite God!

When Satan chose to consider himself worthy of worship and was thrown out of heaven, he lost his revelatory privilege. In other words, he is no longer learning about God. If he were privy to the continual revealing of God's nature, he would have never fallen for the plan of the Cross.

1 Corinthians 2:7-8
But we impart a secret and hidden wisdom of God,
which God decreed before the ages for our glory. None
of the rulers of this age understood this, for if they
had, they would not have crucified the Lord of glory.

Simply, had Satan understood the plan of the Cross, he would have done everything in his power to protect Jesus from it.

Let's take another look at our Scripture from Ephesians.

> *Ephesians 3:10*
>
> *So that **through the church the manifold wisdom of God** might now **be made known to the rulers and authorities in the heavenly places.***

Since Satan is left outside of the revelation of God to the Heavenly host, he is left to discover new elements of God's goodness through... us.

As you receive and respond to fresh revelations of God's goodness, Satan is left to discover the new revelations through your response to them. You're putting him at a tactical disadvantage because he doesn't know this about God and has no prepared response.

Revelation leaves hell defenseless.

This powerful truth should set the hearts of believers aflame with a passion for connecting in intimacy with Jesus and for being equipped with revelatory strategies the enemy has no response for.

Let me explain it one more way.

Bill Johnson from Bethel Church in Redding, California, shared this thought, and it is astounding.

When Solomon was building the temple, he sent letters requesting lumber from another king.

> *1 Kings 5:3-5*
>
> *"You know that David my father could not build a house for the name of the Lord his God because of the warfare with which his enemies surrounded him until the Lord put them under the soles of his feet. **But now the Lord my God has given me rest on every side. There is neither adversary nor misfortune.** And so*

*I intend to build a house for the name of the Lord my
God, as the Lord said to David my father, 'Your son,
whom I will set on your throne in your place, shall
build the house for my name.'"*

His request contains a fascinating statement. *There is neither
adversary nor misfortune.* The Hebrew Word for adversary is *satan.*

Solomon, the type of heavenly wisdom, declared that he had no
adversary or satan

As Johnson put it, wisdom has no satan.[21]

Think of this for a moment. Ephesians 3:10 says that the manifold
wisdom of God is revealed through us to the rulers and authorities. A
simple search through Scripture will show that rulers and authorities
are another way of saying the hosts of hell.

As you and I step into wisdom and revelation, there is no adversary
to that wisdom and revelation.

Amazing! Suddenly "more than conquerors" makes a bit more
sense.

We tend to think that when Jesus said He was going to build
His church and the gates of hell wouldn't prevail against it, Jesus
was talking about hell's offensive weaponry. However, gates are not
offensive; they are defensive. Jesus said He would build His church,
and hell would have no defence against it.

COME OUT HERE – FAITH THAT LOOKS

In the Gospel of Matthew, after Jesus fed the five thousand, He
sent the disciples to the other side of the sea. Jesus then catches up
to them later that evening by walking on the water, frightening the
disciples. After telling them to calm down, Peter pipes up, and because
of the experience he's about to have, we learn a lesson about faith.

Matthew 14:28-31

And Peter answered Him, "Lord, if it is you, command me to come to you on the water." He said, "Come." So Peter exited the boat, walked on the water, and came to Jesus. But when he saw the wind, he was afraid, and beginning to sink, he cried out, "Lord, save me." Jesus immediately reached out His hand and took hold of him, saying to him, "O you of little faith, why did you doubt?"

I used to read this passage thinking Jesus was condescendingly scolding Peter for his lack of faith. But the Lord brought something to my understanding when He reminded me of an overlooked part of this moment from Mark's Gospel.

When Peter's gaze left Jesus, and he began to look at his circumstances, the sheer impossibility of it all started to hit him, and then seeing the wind and the waves, Peter's fear and doubt began to take over.

In a sense, when Jesus reached out to pull Peter up when he began to sink, Jesus said, "Why did you doubt? I am the One who called you out here."

Mark 6:48

*And he saw that they were **making headway painfully**, **for the wind was against them**. And about the fourth watch of the night He came to them, walking on the sea. **He meant to pass by them.***

This is a vital part of radical obedience. I don't think that Jesus was angry at Peter, and the fact that He was going to pass by them to meet them on the other side, proves it. Think of it from Mark's telling of the moment. Why would Jesus leave them in the wind and waves and walk right by them to meet them on the other side?

Because Jesus said that He would meet them on the other side.

And if Jesus said He would meet them there, they would get there. And no storm, no wind, no waves, no NOTHING could prevent them from getting there because Jesus said He would meet them there. So why would He need to stop? If Jesus said He would be there to meet them, it makes sense for Him to get there before the disciples.

When we shift into the sixth gear of radical obedience, we find peace by gazing at Jesus. Not looking at the circumstances, not worrying about outcomes, but with thanksgiving and rejoicing with a faith that looks at the One who can do abundantly more than we could ask or imagine.

Now, I must share an important truth with you in this gear of radical obedience. It is radical obedience, not radical faith. Many will step out in radical faith and fail because they may be operating in belief, but they aren't doing what God asks. Instead, they hope to coerce God into extending His favour and power, by walking in radical faith.

Again, that form of faith depends on an outcome for inner peace. I have ministered to many disappointed saints, who have stepped out in faith, but didn't have Jesus out on the water telling them to join Him there.

Let me use Peter again as an example of the difference between radical obedience and radical faith.

John 21:3-8

Simon Peter said to them, "I am going fishing." *They said to him, "We will go with you." They went out and got into the boat, but that night they caught nothing.*

Just as day was breaking, Jesus stood on the shore; yet the disciples did not know that it was Jesus. Jesus said to them, "Children, do you have any fish?" They answered

Him, "No." He said to them, "Cast the net on the right
side of the boat, and you will find some." So they cast
it, and now they were not able to haul it in, because of
the quantity of fish. That disciple whom Jesus loved
therefore said to Peter, "It is the Lord!" When
Simon Peter heard that it was the Lord, he put on
his outer garment, for he was stripped for work, and
threw himself into the sea. The other disciples came in
the boat, dragging the net full of fish, for they were not
far from the land, but about a hundred yards off.

Here is a question for you. How often do people put more clothes
on to go swimming?

Dr. Randy Clark shared this truth with me once, pointing to the
difference between radical obedience and the danger of radical faith.

He shared (and I agree with him), that Peter had put on his outer
garment because he recalled that the last time he was in a boat and saw
Jesus, he walked on the water to Him.

Radical faith will assume that God will meet you with His power
when you take radical steps of faith. Well, that sounds very wonderful
and charismatic, except, in Peter's case, it resulted in what I think was
a surprising swim.

Why? Because this time, as opposed to Matthew 14:29, Peter
lacked one important thing—Jesus didn't say, "Come."

Radical faith outside of obedience assumes to draw on the power
of God, whereas radical obedience receives a mandate from God to
draw on His power. Now there are many radical steps of obedience
given to us as disciples in God's Word. Praying for the sick, raising
the dead, casting out demons, and works of righteousness, ought to be
pursued because we have God's mandate for them. But the personal

revelatory steps we're discussing in this gear of radical obedience are birthed in intimacy, not out of personal agenda. If it were that way, God would be left to simply supernaturally respond to the individual whims of whatever a believer desires, even if their heart isn't fully submitted.

> *Radical obedience is God's invitation to join Him in overcoming the impossible.*

Radical obedience will always require faith, but radical faith doesn't always require obedience, and that's why it is dangerous to simply think that a radical step of faith will allow you to walk on water outside of the invitation of Jesus.

Radical obedience will be most fulfilling when Jesus remains clearly in charge and in view as we step into impossibility. Radical obedience is God's invitation to join Him in overcoming the impossible.

ROY AND JESSICA'S STORY

Earlier, I shared Roy's story of learning how to manage liberty. His journey through the *Gears of Grace* led to his, and his wife Jessica's, story of radical obedience.

Our journey started with radical obedience in the spring of 1999, when Roy asked me to be his wife after only knowing each other for a grand total of five-and-a-half months.

Many close to us had doubts, but we were committed to each other, knowing that God had set us apart for each other, and six months later, on November 6, 1999, we were married.

Days after the wedding, we moved 500 miles north to Roy's hometown of La Crete, Alberta. We were happy there, and I worked hard to fit into the traditional Mennonite way of life, which was a stretch for me coming from a Pentecostal background.

Roy grew up farming and farmed alongside his second youngest brother. They were both hard-working and focused, but Roy had always felt a tug on his heart to explore life beyond his roots. Because I was the type of girl who always felt like I had a bit of a hippie soul – exploring life beyond the confines of 'life as usual' seemed noble and free. We decided it was worth taking a chance to sell out of the farm, sell the home we had lived in for two years and move south.

Over the next ten years, with three wonderful children, many pets, and twelve moves worth of moving boxes, we did our best to follow God's promptings as we knew they would propel us into the destiny He had set before us. Each move was not void of difficulties, disappointments, tears shed, or hearts needing to be mended occasionally. But it was full of the promise of something more that He was bringing us into. It challenged us to be brave and to reinvent ourselves each time. We were truly walking in being transformed from glory to glory (2 Cor. 3:18). The radical obedience we had said yes to twelve years prior was something we had continued to say yes to year after year.

Not too long ago, the Holy Spirit spoke these words to me, "Obedience is an act of the will, whereas surrender is an act of the heart." When we are submitted wholeheartedly to the Father, we trust His good intentions for our life; we tend not to worry and fret over the outcome. We then enter a place of rest where we begin to walk hand in hand with Him knowing that we are safe in the requests He makes to us.

However, after a very fruitful season in our lives of being healthy as a family, moving forward in our business, and being planted firmly in our church, our understanding of radical obedience was about to grow dramatically.

In the late spring of 2015, the Holy Spirit dropped into my heart that we were to home-school our three children the following school year. At the time, Isabelle was heading into 9th grade, Carmen into 7th grade, and our son Micael into 5th grade. I wasn't ready for a task that size. Homeschooling was certainly not in my plans for the year, but I knew He had a plan, and we agreed to follow Him.

As spring approached, I remember feeling something was taking place in my spirit. I couldn't quite put my finger on what it was, but I shared with Roy that it felt like the Lord was shaking the foundations of our lives. While we couldn't quite define it, we knew it was significant. The summer months rolled on, and the shaking process continued. As fall approached and the start of the school year just around the corner, we began to gather our materials and set up our classroom.

The closer we got to school starting, the more unqualified and unprepared I felt. However, two things kept me from completely losing my cool. The first was the support I had from Roy, and the second was my faith in God's promises that he had spoken to my spirit. With those two things on my side, I forged ahead in obedience.

In the first week of September 2015, the Holy Spirit began to speak to me while getting ready for the upcoming school day. He playfully said, "I want to give you a heads-up on your word for 2016." You see, at the start of each New Year, I ask the Holy Spirit to give me a word for the upcoming year. It seemed exciting and strange that He wanted to share this year's word with me so early.

"Your word for 2016 is Adventure, and you will move to Phoenix."

And I thought that homeschooling was a big task! To be honest, at that moment, I wasn't immediately excited. Instead, I felt intimidated and fearful. However, I could feel in my spirit that this was not a suggestion from Him or something He even wanted us to consider prayerfully, but there was a radical urgency behind what He was saying. I responded, "I feel terrified and apprehensive, but if you ask us to do this, I trust you."

When I called Roy to tell him what I'd heard the Holy Spirit say to me, his response was priceless. "It's about time!" he exclaimed. His answer made sense because we had businesses in Phoenix for quite a few years and had vacationed there a few times. Roy and the kids loved the weather. However, I didn't appreciate the heat. Frankly, I loved my home in Canada and couldn't imagine moving away from there. On one of those vacations, Roy asked if I would ever consider moving to Phoenix. I said that the Lord would have to ask me to do it. My saying that provided an open door of permission for my Father to ask that very thing.

We called a family meeting and shared with the kids what we had heard God say and that we would obey Him. Because they trusted us and Jesus, they became excited along with us and were up for this new adventure. We began to pack up our dream home and had all of our life's belongings packed and ready to go three weeks later.

We set out towards the border with a sense of peace, knowing that we were in His will and that He was pleased with the radical step of obedience we had taken.

However, we didn't know that there was about to be a challenge on that obedience shortly.

When we arrived at the border crossing, the officer had a few concerns and asked us to come into their office for further questioning. At the desk, they told us they had questions concerning the visas for our kids. Roy had already received a visa in the fall of 2014 because he often travelled back and forth on business. Our attorney added me to Roy's visa, but our kids had no visa documentation. He told us that they would only travel for vacation since they were all under 18. Because of that, we were told they didn't need visas but could come under our jurisdiction.

Unfortunately, the counsel we received was wrong, and as a result, they couldn't let us across the border into the US and told us that we would have to turn around.

We were shocked. Roy and I chatted, wondering what we were going to do. Then a boldness rose in me, and I told Roy, "God is the one who has called us to this place, so He will be the one to fix this and get us across." As Roy returned to the desk, one of the female officers came over to see what was happening. Since we had already been there for 2 hours, she wondered why this was taking so long.

She asked her colleague about the problem, and he told her about the visa situation with our kids. Then she asked us one question that changed everything.

"Are you enrolling the kids in the public school system?"

We said they would be home-schooled, and her response was our first miracle! She told the other officer to stamp our passports and give the kids six months to get their proper documentation and let us cross! God moved radically on our behalf, and in two months, we had all of our documents in place for each of the kids, and our adventure had begun.

That first miracle has become a defining moment for us. To think that the first task of homeschooling would be the reason we would be able to step into the next step of obedience. It moved us from simply trusting Him to a deeper level of faith in His power to move Heaven and earth to accomplish His will and purposes for our lives.

Faith becomes the nucleus of radical obedience when we are tested in the fire. It holds the promise of tomorrow and gives us peace, which sustains us in times of testing.

Our radical step of obedience has had its share of challenges, but there have been so many blessings. Our businesses have both flourished and expanded. The move also opened up to me (Jessica) business oppor-

tunities that are God-ordained, and I am getting to influence many key business-people in the region. Our lives have become so filled with purpose and impact that we continually find ourselves amazed at God's faithfulness and favour!

For us, there has been no greater adventure to be lived on this side of Heaven than to walk in the way of radical obedience. It has pushed us out of the mould we can so quickly put ourselves into and propelled us into a life of no limits with Him. Now we find ourselves asking, "What's next, Lord?"

THE FRUIT OF INTIMACY – WHISPERS OR COMMANDS

Can you see how intimacy was the birthing place for radical obedience in Roy and Jessica's story? As Jessica spent time close to Jesus, He whispered destiny into her heart.

This gear of radical obedience is realized as a fruit of intimacy with Jesus. Simply because we walk in what we heard Him say to us in the secret places of our hearts. Radical obedience is not born out of any other place but intimacy.

To be driven by any other source than simply obeying God is to put ourselves at risk of slipping into radical faith. Need or passion mustn't drive us. Gifting or anointing will not be sufficient to lead us. Position and authority will not be enough to sustain us. The word that God gave us to step out on the water will activate His supernatural response to our faith-filled steps of radical obedience.

While God will resort to having to command us as His disciples to a task on occasion, his preference is to whisper to us as His beloved. Any general can command an uninterested, perhaps even an unwilling, soldier into battle out of fear of retribution. But our King would instead whisper into the souls of His beloved; those ones who have caught His heart and are willing to act because of their love for their sweet King. A general may be able to force soldiers to a task because of his positional authority. But sweet Jesus would rather have a relationship with you, resulting in acts from shared passion.

ONE LAST WORD ON FAITH – SIMPLIFY

As I have observed and participated in radical obedience, one thing about the faith we step into is that it needs to be simple. The bigger the task, the simpler the faith.

> *Matthew 17:19-20*
>
> *Then the disciples came to Jesus privately and said, "Why could we not cast it out?" He said to them, "Because of your little faith. For truly, I say to you, if you have faith like a grain of mustard seed, you will say to this mountain, 'Move from here to there,' and it will move, and nothing will be impossible for you."*

In the above scripture, Jesus points to the kind of faith that believes in the power that's made available when He mandates us to a task. The larger the task, the more committed we must be to trust that He has the power to see us through it.

Remember, the anchor of great faith is that God had the power to raise Jesus from the dead. If you believe in the gospel, you possess the faith you need to move mountains. Faith is not a feeling. We can't muster up feeling enough faith to be obedient; instead, be obedient and act in faith, believing that God will cause the water to hold us up since He commanded us to come out there in the first place.

CLUTCH PRAYER – REPENT

Lord Jesus, thank You for Your love, grace, and power. I declare in Your Name that I possess the faith I need to see mountains move. I possess the faith I need to radically obey You when You speak to my heart. I repent for doubt and worry and reject their influence on my obedience. I ask that You wrap me in Your peace, so I would rest in Your goodness and trust Your promise never to leave or forsake me when I am stepping out in obedience to Your call.

I choose to trust You and follow You. Open my ears to hear Your voice, my eyes to see Your ways, and my heart to know Your peace.

I love you.

In Jesus' name,

Amen

A Quick Review

The sixth Gear of Grace, is Radical Obedience—lives of impact.

The tension is the size of the task.

The clutch is faith—believing in the power that is available to you.

The clutch of faith allows you to move from one act of impact to another as the Holy Spirit leads you.

STUDY QUESTIONS

If you are in a group study, share some testimonies of when you have walked in Radical Obedience?

What areas have you experienced a revelation that empowered you to walk in a greater anointing?

How can you guard yourself against walking in radical faith ahead of radical obedience?

Renew - How is the Holy Spirit challenging your trust levels with God through opportunities for Radical Obedience? (Remember, the renewal of our mind is learning what heaven says about a thing and making that the truth we live in.)

Respond - In what ways do you hear God calling you to step out of the boat and start walking on the water? (Reread Come Out Here-Faith That Looks)

CHAPTER 10

CONCLUSION

THE GEARS AND LIFE

> *Ephesians 4:15*
> *Rather, speaking the truth in love, we are to grow up*
> *in every way into Him who is the Head, into Christ.*

AS OUR JOURNEY TOGETHER COMES TO A CLOSE, YOU MIGHT find yourself frustrated, and a little confused because as you take inventory of your life. You may feel like you are in third gear in one area, first gear in another, and fourth in yet another place, and perhaps not know what to do about it.

Good.

That is part of the purpose of writing Gears of Grace. To challenge us in the areas of our lives where we are compartmentalizing and walking in a stunted form of faith. Perhaps you are looking at your business, or family life, and seeing the gear you are living in there. Or maybe it is in your marriage or friendships that you see yourself walking in a lower gear. Or maybe different secret areas of your heart are still stuck in immature gears.

Wherever you may be feeling the tension, I join Paul's challenge to you from Ephesians 4:15 shared at the beginning of this chapter to *"grow up in every way into him who is the head, into Christ."*

Your first and most important response to this book is to allow the Holy Spirit to take a spiritual inventory of your life and invite Him to show you where you are in lower gears.

Then it becomes your choice whether you want to face the tension and implement the clutch to move forward.

The essential and vital thing you can bring — to your destiny, relationships, family, career, and church — is the healthiest you.

This is where remembering the two levels of discipleship can be of value. In some areas, you may need to consciously return to the first level of deliberate submission to the Lordship of Jesus to begin establishing the necessary thought patterns that will move you forward in maturity in those areas. As you do that, you will find the strength to grow out of immaturity and into wholeness in your life's broken or stunted areas and move forward in your faith.

Your first and most important response to this book is to allow the Holy Spirit to take a spiritual inventory of your life and invite Him to show you where you are in lower gears.

Or perhaps through your growth in intimacy with Jesus, learn the kingdom way and move forward in seeing desires fulfilled and dreams realized.

Each gear holds value because it is an expression of God's grace. But living primarily in first and second gear blocks the disciple from engaging a faith that has meaningful impact and fulfilment. However, first and second gear both remain wonderful gifts to even the mature believer.

> *Hebrews 4:16*
> ***Let us then with confidence draw near to the throne of grace, that we may receive mercy and find grace to help in time of need.***

The fact is that no one could drive a vehicle without the first three gears. And there will be times when we need, without fear of retribution or condemnation, to return to first gear and receive our guaranteed forgiveness for sin. Or to return to second gear and establish or reestablish our discipline in an area. Occasionally, a hill may be long or steep, and we will need to downshift to make it through.

God is OK with that.

At the same time, we don't return to lower gears to simply live there again but to be empowered by them, to reengage higher gears so we can live at destiny speed.

Writing this book was born out of a desire for people to identify where they are in their maturity and equip them with tools to move forward and mature. So often, we're told to mature, but we are unsure where or how.

I pray that within the pages of Gears of Grace, you have greater clarity about your personal maturity in your walk with Jesus and have found the necessary tools to move forward, mature, and live at the Speed of Destiny!

Appendix

Three Laws of New Testament Belief

The Law of Faith – Justification

Romans 3:27-28

Then what becomes of our boasting? It is excluded. By what kind of law? By a law of works? No, but by the law of faith. For we hold that one is justified by faith apart from works of the law.

According to the law of faith, we're not allowed to use religiosity to justify us, but only through the work of the Cross. Paul's declaration in Galatians confirms this.

Galatians 2:16

Yet we know that a person is not justified by works of the law but through faith in Jesus Christ, so we also have believed in Christ Jesus, in order to be justified by faith in Christ and not by works of the law, because by works of the law no one will be justified.

Now we must recognize the tension that this law embraces. Righteous acts without true faith in Jesus will not justify anyone. However, faith without righteous deeds is dead, according to James.

James 2:20-26

*Do you want to be shown, you foolish person, **that faith apart from works is useless?** Was not **Abraham our father justified by works** when he offered up his son Isaac on the altar? You see that **faith was active along with his works, and faith was completed by his works;** and the Scripture was fulfilled that says, **"Abraham believed God, and it was counted to him as righteousness"**—and he was called a friend of God. You see that a person is **justified by works and not by faith alone.** And in the same way was not also Rahab the prostitute justified by works when she received the messengers and sent them out by another way? For as **the body apart from the spirit is dead, so also faith apart from works is dead.***

While appearing to be in contradiction, they complement each other. And Jesus shows us how.

Matthew 5:16

*"In the same way, **let your light shine before others,** so that they **may see your good works and give glory to your Father who is in Heaven."***

Any righteous work done to somehow earn our own righteous standing before the Lord violates the law of faith. But, at the same time, our faith will result in works done, not to justify ourselves as an act of our worthiness but as an act of worship.

So, the law of faith protects us from the spirit of religion corrupting our rela-

> *Any righteous work done to somehow earn our own righteous standing before the Lord violates the law of faith.*

tionship with God while at the same time guarding us from slothful disobedience to His call to action.

THE LAW OF THE SPIRIT

Romans 8:1-2

*There is **therefore now no condemnation** for those who are in Christ Jesus. **For the law of the Spirit of life has set you free** in Christ Jesus from the law of sin and death.*

According to the law of the Spirit, it is not lawful to live under condemnation. What a fantastic law! It is illegal to live under condemnation. The law of faith and the law of the Spirit work hand in hand in this fashion. Your works do not justify you; if you feel condemned because of something you have done, you can't earn back good standing. By faith, you receive your justification, and in being led by the Spirit, you receive the necessary blueprint to live outside of any condemnation.

Jesus confirmed this when He described the work of the Spirit on behalf of His disciples in John's Gospel.

John 16:8-11

*And when he comes, **he will convict the world concerning sin and righteousness and judgment:** concerning sin, because they do not believe in me; concerning righteousness, because I go to the Father, and you will see me no longer; concerning judgment, because the ruler of this world is judged.*

The Holy Spirit's work for the believer is defined at the beginning of verse ten. Convicting means to bring to the light. He isn't convicting disciples as we would look at a judge convicting for punishment. Instead, he is bringing to light what righteousness, which is our condition because of the law of faith, looks like in every situation so that we are well-equipped and led to show forth the righteousness of Jesus to the world.

In other words, He will say to you, "This is how the righteous respond." And you are invited to follow His lead.

Listed below are some of the benefits of the law of the Spirit:

Baptism– Mark 1:8, Acts 1:5, Acts 2:1-4
Power– Acts 1:8
Freedom– Romans 8:2
Life and Peace– Romans 8:6
Identity– Romans 8:15
Inheritance– Romans 8:16
Gifts– 1 Corinthians 12,14
Fruit– Galatians 5:22-25

The law of the Spirit embraces tension as well. The law of the Spirit protects us from condemnation from the enemy but also moves us away from fleshly living. We see it in Romans 8.

Romans 8:3-9

> For **God has done what the law,** weakened by the **flesh, could not do.** By sending His own Son in the likeness of sinful flesh and for sin, He condemned sin in the flesh, **in order that the righteous requirement of the law might be fulfilled in us, who walk not according to the flesh but according to the Spirit.** For those who live according to the flesh set their minds on the things of the flesh, but those

The law of the Spirit protects us from condemnation from the enemy but also moves us away from fleshly living.

who live according to the Spirit set their minds on
the things of the Spirit. For to set the mind on the
flesh is death, but to set the mind on the Spirit is
life and peace. For the mind that is set on the flesh is
hostile to God, for it does not submit to God's law;
indeed, it cannot. Those who are in the flesh cannot
please God. You, however, are not in the flesh but
in the Spirit, if in fact the Spirit of God dwells in you.
Anyone who does not have the Spirit of Christ does not
belong to Him.

And again, in Galatians.

Galatians 5:16-18

*But I say, **walk by the Spirit,** and you will **not gratify***
the desires of the flesh. For the desires of the flesh are
against the Spirit, and the desires of the Spirit are
*against the flesh, for these are **opposed to each other,***
to keep you from doing the things you want to do. But if
*you are **led by the Spirit, you are not under the law.***

So, the law of the Spirit will protect us from living under the condemnation and guilt sown by the accuser of the brethren (Satan) while at the same time leading and guiding us into all truth.

John 16:13

*When the Spirit of Truth comes, He **will guide you***
into all the truth, for He will not speak on His own
authority, but whatever He hears He will speak, and
He will declare to you the things that are to come.

THE ROYAL LAW – LOVE

James 2:8

*If you really **fulfill the royal law** according to the Scripture, "You shall love your neighbour as yourself," you are doing well.*

According to the royal law, love for others helps us do well. The royal law is what most represents the nature of the King and His Kingdom.

1 John 4:7-8

*Beloved, **let us love one another**, for love is from God, and **whoever loves has been born of God** and knows God. Anyone **who does not love does not know God**, because **God is love**.*

Many teachers believe that when the children of Israel were in the desert, they didn't take their initial opportunity to enter the Promised Land because of their slave mentality. They would say that Moses remained the leader of the next generation because he wasn't born into slavery but raised as royalty. Their enslaved mindset resulted in a generation of enslaved people dying in the desert so that a generation of children of the promise could take the land.

Today, amongst some, "Your Kingdom come," means the earthly dominion of the Body of Christ over the world. As if legislating righteousness to force people into a Kingdom mindset would be God's preferred ideal. This isn't true. The King of this Kingdom will rule, and He presently is absolutely sovereign. However, He is not exercising control as if to establish a police state. On the contrary, he takes our free will very seriously and will not violate that until He has deemed it is time to establish His tangible reign.

Galatians 4:28
Now you, brothers, like Isaac, are children of promise.

I'm sharing this with you because we are royalty. After all, we are freeborn according to the law of liberty. However, our representation of what royalty is supposed to look like is not what the world would know royalty to be.

Proverbs 30:21-23
Under three things the earth trembles;
under four it cannot bear up:
a slave when he becomes king,
and a fool when he is filled with food;
an unloved woman when she gets a husband,
and a maidservant when she displaces her mistress.

There is nothing more dangerous than when slaves become kings. When an enslaved mindset is brought into royalty, it will only give authority to self-gratification. Slave-kings live to only protect what they have and try to get more regardless of the cost to others and will live in constant fear of what they have being taken away.

Mark 10:42-45
*And Jesus called them to Him and said to them, "You know that **those who are considered rulers of the Gentiles lord it over them, and their great ones exercise authority over them. But it shall not be so among you.** But whoever would be **great among you must be your servant,** and whoever **would be first among you must be slave of all.** For even the **Son of Man came not to be served but to serve,** and to give His life as a ransom for many."*

Jesus throws the gauntlet down to His disciples and says, you have seen it done from the top down, but that's not how it will be with us; leaders will serve, royalty will care about the people in the Kingdom above the riches of the Kingdom.

Jesus' example of royal love wasn't to preserve His Kingdom but to give it away.

Think of it from the perspective of relationships. You can serve without love, discipline without love, correct without love, provide without love, communicate without love, and even be intimate without love. But you can't love without service, discipline, correction, provision, communication, and intimacy.

The tension of this law is living positionally as royalty and yet practically as servants.

It is illegal in the Kingdom to operate outside of love.

*It is illegal in the Kingdom
to operate outside of love.*

REFERENCES

[1] All Bible references are from the English Standard Version (ESV) unless otherwise stated.

[2] Alan Hirsch and Darryn Altclass, *The Forgotten Way Handbook* (Grand Rapids, MI: Brazos Press, 2009), 37.

[3] Malcom Smith, *The Power of the Blood Covenant: Uncover the Secret Strength of God's Eternal Oath* (Tulsa, OK: Harrison House Publishers, 2002), 13.

[4] Smith, *Blood Covenant*, 75.

[5] Smith, *Blood Covenant*, 13.

[6] Smith, *Blood Covenant*, 16-17.

[7] Smith, *Blood Covenant*, 94.

[8] John C. Maxwell, *The 21 Irrefutable Laws of Leadership* (HarperCollins Leadership, 2007). p 8

[9] Not all scholars agree that agape and phileo hold different meanings however, the fact that the writer recorded Jesus using the two different words point to the importance of the difference between the two. As a result I am comfortable considering the nuanced difference in the words.

[10] Alan Hirsch and Darryn Altclass, The Forgotten Way Handbook (Grand Rapids, MI: Brazos Press, 2009), 37.

[11] W.E. Vine, Merrill F. Unger and William White Jr, *An Expository Dictionary of Biblical Words,* (Nashville, TN: Thomas Nelson Publishers, 1984), 733.

[12] Charles R. Swindoll, *The Grace Awakening,* (Dallas, TX: Word Publishing, 1996), 43.

[13] Tony Stoltzfus, Questions for Jesus, (Redding, CA: Coach 22 Bookstore LLC, 2013), 7.

[14] Stoltzfus, Questions, 7.

[15] Bill Johnson, *Experience the Impossible* (Bloomington, MN: Chosen, 2014), 34.

[16] H. D. McDonald, "Apollinarianism," ed. Martin Davie et al., *New Dictionary of Theology: Historical and Systematic* (London; Downers Grove, IL: Inter-Varsity Press; InterVarsity Press, 2016), 48.

[17] Stoltzfus, Questions, 7. (Italics mine)

[18] Garry Lefebvre, "David Mainse Interviews Garry Lefebvre," Garry Lefebvre | 10 Huntly Street, July 22, 2002, posted on Promotions, March 22, 2016, online video, https://www.youtube.com/watch?v=5XewRSZsElE&t=17s; you can see the actual interview here, 1973 CFL Grey Cup Edmonton Eskimos vs Ottawa Rough Riders CBC Original, posted on Newton Minnowowski, May 22, 2018, online video, https://www.youtube.com/watch?v=A-Hm-SuGzPG4, 3:27:32.

[19] Kathryn Kuhlman, "How to Be Filled and Controlled by the Holy Spirit," online, YouTube, 10 min mark, https://youtu.be/jJhGX-CRJEqM.

[20] Jake Hayford, "Why you need to be filled with the Holy Spirit," online, Jack Hayford Legacy Library Channel, YouTube, April 28, 2017, https://www.youtube.com/watch?v=waJRjrmFoz0once.

[21] Bill Johnson, "Wisdom Has No Adversary," online, *Online-Sermons.org*, October 3, 2021, https://online-sermons.org/billjohnson/4813-bill-johnson-wisdom-has-no-adversary.html.

About the Author

Rev. Landen Dorsch began his first ministry assignment in 1996 in a small church called Gospel Chapel in Sylvan Lake, Alberta. He served as an assistant pastor overseeing worship and youth ministry. After a healthy and vibrant season of ministry at Gospel Chapel, he and his family embarked upon their second ministry assignment at Eagles Nest Ranch, nestled in the Cypress Hills south of Medicine Hat, Alberta.

As executive director, Landen led a team of one hundred staff at the summer camp for at-risk kids and teens. During their summer camping season, Landen and his team used dynamic worship, creative themes, and activities to draw youth into a saving knowledge of Jesus. Throughout his time at Eagles Nest, Landen saw thousands of kids and teens impacted by the gospel.

When his season ended at Eagles Nest Ranch, Landen and his family returned to the Edmonton area, where he grew up, to pastor Gateway Family Church in Leduc. He continues to lead that church at the time of this writing.

Along with being the Lead Pastor at Gateway, Landen travels as a guest speaker and mentor for leaders, serves on several ministry leadership boards, continues to write, and hosts a hunting show called Kingdom Wild on WildTV, which airs across Canada.

Landen has the heart of a worshipper. He is an insightful, anointed communicator and a gifted worship leader passionate about seeing God's family enter His presence. At the core of his ministry, Landen models empowerment and pursues facilitating the destiny of those he leads. With a message of hope, Landen challenges and encourages the body of Christ to enter into the fullness of God's Kingdom.

Landen and his wife Cathy have four children—Alyssa and her husband Brody, Tyler and his wife Robin, Amy-Lynn, and Jenna, along with two amazing grandsons, Callum and Silas, and a third grandchild in the way. As a family, they are all committed to seeing God's kingdom advance through themselves and those they lead: he and his family love to laugh and enjoy being in Christ-centred community.

Landen is an Ordained Minister in the Pentecostal Assemblies of Canada.

For more information about Landen, Gateway Family Church, or Kingdom Wild, or to contact Landen or Gateway, visit their websites:

WWW.GATEWAYFAMILY.CA

WWW.KINGDOMWILD.TV

Thank you for completing *Gears of Grace*.

We would love if you could help by posting a review at your book retailer and on the PageMaster Publishing site. It only takes a minute and it would really help others by giving them an idea of your experience.

Thanks

Landen Dorsch at the Pagemaster Publishing Store

https://pagemasterpublishing.ca/by/landen-dorsch/

To order more copies of this book, find books by other Canadian authors, or make inquiries about publishing your own book, contact PageMaster at:

PageMaster Publication Services Inc.
11340-120 Street, Edmonton, AB T5G 0W5
books@pagemaster.ca
780-425-9303

catalogue and e-commerce store
PageMasterPublishing.ca/Shop

ENDORSEMENTS

I so enjoy seeing Landen put what he lives on paper. In *Gears of Grace* he provides an intentional pathway to growth – growth as people, and as leaders towards a life of fruitfulness and purpose. Landen is not afraid to point out the obstacles that would restrict us from changing gears and growing, and the beautiful thing is, he and I have had many deep conversations where we prayerfully explore obstacles together. This has led to personal breakthrough! Landen is a pastor, leader, father and friend and *Gears of Grace* pushes you forward step by step, gear by gear from each of those perspectives. It is a book worth reading, and a book worth reading with a friend.

Darcy McAlister
Global Worker in Asia
Pentecostal Assemblies of Canada

"Gears of Grace" offers fresh perspectives that will enlighten your spiritual journey. As Landen walks you through the book, you will have a fresh revelation of the measure of grace that is available to each of us. This book is a must read for both new converts and more mature believers.

Dr. Tom Jones
Executive VP of Global Awakening

At first, *Gears of Grace*, Landen Dorsch's new book, seemed like an odd title to me. Perhaps he meant to write years of grace or tears of grace. What could Gears of Grace mean? As I read the book, it became clear to me that God had given Landen insight into grace and living a victorious Christian life from his experience driving a car through multiple gears.

His metaphor is actually a great one to help people understand the biblical concepts for a victorious Christian life. Landen points out that you cannot achieve highway speed in first gear. In order to reach a faster speed or destiny speed, you have to move through the gears. The ultimate desire is to fulfill heaven's destiny for your life and to live a victorious life rather than a defeated or mediocre life for Christ.

He explains how the resistance you feel in your life is a sign you need to shift gears. In this analogy, Landen points out what is needed to do so. Now, moving to a car's stick shift, he introduces the concept of the clutch. He then points out how to know it is time to shift and what is required to engage the clutch to get to the next gear. Each gear represents growth in Christ and some of the issues one faces in that season of being conformed to the image of Christ. I so appreciate the balance of this book. The true biblical perspective on grace keeps us out of the two temptations or deceptions of hyper-grace or sloppy grace and religious legalism or works-based acceptance. Landen points out the difference between working or obeying from love and working or obeying for love.

Landen, a seasoned pastor, and one of my best students at Global Awakening Theological Seminary, has lots of illustrations from his life as a pastor and a strong solid theology. One of his statements, which I thoroughly enjoyed and was blessed by, was related to his first experience as a teenage church camp counselor. A young girl manifested a demon, she did not know Landen, but the demon called out his name. This unnerved Landen, "They know who I am in hell." Then the Lord communicated to Landen, "Landen, if they don't know you in hell, you mustn't be doing much for Heaven. Take it as a compliment. Hell is intimidated by you." This illustration comes from the discussion of third gear, where the believer learns more about his or her authority in Christ.

But it is not enough to learn about one's authority, the need is to have enough faith to exercise it. Landen is not giving us some esoteric gnostic-laden formula about how to progress up the ladder to oneness with a non-personal god that is the life force of all that exists. He is not a new-ager. Instead, his book is rooted in Jesus and His cross. It is a book about grace and the power of the Holy Spirit. I don't want to give too much away.

I hope you will buy and read the *Gears of Grace* and discover in what gear your life is being lived. Also, apply the biblical truths to come into your full destiny. There is good biblical theology in what Landen has written. Apply the truth to your life, and may any and all deceptions of the enemy be exposed so you may live in the freedom of the truth. May your name become known in hell because you're in-fluencing the population of heaven and advancing God's Kingdom on the earth, as a result of your application of the truth in *Gears of Grace*.

Dr. Randy Clark
D.D., D.Min., Th.D., M.Div., B.S. Religious Studies
Overseer of the apostolic network of Global Awakening
President of Global Awakening Theological Seminary
amazon.com/author/randyclark

Have you ever experienced growing pains? They can occur in our bodies, businesses, ministries, and life stages. They occur in the stages of Christian growth toward maturity as well. What are the signs? Why is it uncomfortable? How do we cooperate rather than resist? My friend and anointed colleague Landen Dorsch tells us in his newest book, *Gears of Grace*. In his characteristic wisdom, wit, and years of experience, Landen helps clear the roadway and speed on toward our destiny in Christ, navigating the speed bumps and avoiding wreckage. He gives us practical counsel and relevant examples, all wrapped in the love and grace of God. Thank God. There is hope for me yet!

Dr. Kim Maas
Founder/CEO Kim Maas Ministries
Author of *Prophetic Community: God's Call For All to Minister in His Gifts* and *The Way of the Kingdom: Seizing the Times For a Great Move of God,* and forthcoming in May 2024, *Finding Our Muchness: Inheriting Audacious Boldness from Women in the Bible.*

Gears of Grace is a must read for anyone craving to be closer to God. Within the following pages, you will discover how God will empower you to overcome challenges too strong for you to overcome on your own. This book will also give you practical steps to position yourself to receive spiritual gifts from God, allowing you to make a powerful, eternal impact on each life you've been divinely assigned to lead.

Frankie Mazzapica
Nationally Televised Speaker, Author,
and Lead Pastor of Celebration Church, The Woodlands, Texas

Unlock the transformative power of God's grace in your life with this remarkable masterpiece. Within the pages of this book, you will embark on a profound journey into the depths of God's unmerited favor, a journey that will awaken your spirit to new dimensions of His love and compassion.

With each turn of the page, you will be swept into a realm where the boundless grace of our Lord flows like a river, erasing every stain of guilt and shame, and embracing you in the arms of His mercy. As you read, your heart will resonate with the heartbeat of heaven, resonating with the truth that you are a beloved child of the King, cherished beyond measure, and fully accepted by the One who is Love Himself.

Prepare to be captivated by the powerful testimonies and revelatory insights that grace this book's sacred pages. Landen Dorsch's unique anointing, cultivated through years of intimacy with the Father, shines through every word, illuminating the path towards a deeper understanding of the grace that sustains and empowers us. Through these profound teachings, you will come to recognize that God's grace is not just a theological concept, but a living force that transforms us from the inside out.

Let the wisdom and revelation in this book lead you into encounters with the God of unfathomable goodness and kindness. May the revelations within these pages open your eyes to the boundless possibilities that unfold when we embrace the grace of God as the foundation of our lives. Get ready to be refreshed, renewed, and equipped to walk in the fullness of God's grace as never before."

Samuel Robinson
President, Voice of Revival and Host of Voice of Revival TV

We are called to live not only within our own potential but live abundant lives that come only from God. We live this life by the grace He has given to us – His followers. Landen does a superb job unpacking what "grace" is by grounding us in the Word of God, imparting practical life principles, and sharing powerful stories to launch us into a higher dimensions of living -living by grace! *Gears of Grace* is a book that will help you go from strength to strength, faith to faith, glory to glory. I highly commend my good friend Landen and recommend this book!

Tony Kim
V.P. Harvest International Ministry

If you are looking for something to help you grow past your current faith plateau, to help you get "unstuck" from a season of disappointment or disillusionment, I believe the words in this book, *Gears of Grace*, will be pivotal in your journey. After walking with Pastor Landen for over 27 years in life and ministry, I have seen him apply these scriptural truths to overcome and remain fruitful in every season. I have had the privilege of growing up under his pastoral leadership and have personally experienced the breakthrough that comes as we press on through the tension, towards the next level of grace, "from glory to glory". There is always more!

Amy Ball
Family Pastor, Gateway Family Church

What if your destiny isn't tied to a destination or an activity, but is tied to the KIND of person you are and the WAY you live? The big idea here is that destiny has more to do with moving with God at His speed and in His strength, what Landen calls the "speed of destiny". This book deals with our small minded understanding of grace and draws us beyond the "to sin or not to sin" discipleship ditch. With practical metaphors, insightful stories, and personal practices for you to engage, this book will help you shift into new mindsets that will bring fruitfulness in and out of season. If you're longing to experience the wholistic transformation that God's Grace truly empowers, then it might be time to shift into the next gear of grace!

Josh Frey
Senior Associate, Gateway Family Church

If you're feeling stalled in your relationship with Jesus, this latest book from Landen Dorsch will take your Christian faith to the next level. Using a simple metaphor of cars and stick shifts, Landen insightfully walks you through an explanation of the different stages -or gears -of the Christian life. If you're spinning the wheels in your faith, Landen reveals the "clutch" in each stage and guides you through the process of shifting into the next gear with Christ. Whether you're a beginner stuck in first gear or a seasoned believer coasting in fourth, Landen takes your spiritual RPMs to the red-line and then helps you shift into the higher gears of your potential.

Ryan Stockert
Thunder And Light Studios
Executive Producer of "KINGDOM WILD"

If you've ever struggled to identify what is stunting your spiritual growth, Landen has written an insightful guide that can help you find the "Gears" to accelerate your walk with God. You don't need to be a car enthusiast to discover great value here. By applying the principles shared in these pages, you'll discover a transformative tool that can help you move forward in a vibrant growing relationship with God.

Kevin Johnson
District Superintendent, Maritime District – PAOC

I love Landen's play on words and this image of gear shifting is a great one. "Gears of Grace" suggests that we can't stay where we are and beckons us to shift into the next assignment God has placed before us. We've all had to apply some mental gear shifting from time to time but this is more than that. This is a call to live out the purpose for which you were created. You have a destiny where you've been called "for such a time as this." Our destiny is highly dependant upon our willingness to move beyond our comfort zone and shift into what God has ordained for us. To settle where we are will only cause us to stagnate and become ineffective for the Kingdom. I love this book for three reasons. It's biblical, It's relatable and it's extremely helpful. I know you'll love it too.

Pastor Mike Love
Senior Pastor, Life Church
President, Extreme Dream Ministries